DISASTERS

CRITICAL READING SERIES

DISASTERS

21 Stories of Death and Destruction—with Exercises for Developing Reading Comprehension and Critical Thinking Skills

Henry Billings
Melissa Billings
Dan Dramer

JAMESTOWN PUBLISHERS

a division of NTC/CONTEMPORARY PUBLISHING GROUP
Lincolnwood, Illinois USA

ISBN 0-89061-112-2

Published by Jamestown Publishers,
a division of NTC/Contemporary Publishing Group, Inc.
4255 West Touhy Avenue
Lincolnwood (Chicago), Illinois 60646-1975, U.S.A.
890 VL 0987654321

CONTENTS

UNIT THREE

To the Student

What is the worst calamity that ever happened to you? Multiply the problems you experienced during that event hundreds of times, and you will get some idea of the suffering that a true disaster brings. Many times, disasters cause misery and death for tens, hundreds, or even thousands of people. Whole cities can be destroyed. When such a huge disaster occurs, it is so different from everyday life that everyone remembers it for a long time. People retell its story over and over again.

Each lesson in this book will introduce you to one of the most famous and memorable disasters ever. The articles have been written in the style of a newspaper or magazine story. They present the facts about the disaster—the people who were affected, the cause of the disaster, and sometimes, the disaster's long-lasting effects. Often, you will get a chance to read the words of people who suffered through the disaster and lived to tell others about it.

As you read and enjoy these articles, you will also be developing your reading skills. *Disasters* is for students who already read fairly well but who want to read faster and to increase their understanding of what they read. If you complete the 21 lessons—reading the articles and completing the exercises—you will surely increase your reading speed and improve your reading comprehension and critical thinking skills. Also, because these exercises include items of the types often found on state and national tests, learning how to complete them will prepare you for tests you may have to take in the future.

How to Use This Book

About the Book. *Disasters* contains three units, each of which includes seven lessons. Each lesson begins with an article about an unusual event, person, or group. The article is followed by a group of four reading comprehension exercises and a set of three critical thinking exercises. The reading comprehension exercises will help you understand the article. The critical thinking exercises will help you think about what you have read and how it relates to your own experience.

At the end of each lesson, you will also have the opportunity to give your personal response to some aspect of the article and then to assess how well you understood what you read.

The Sample Lesson.   Working through the sample lesson, the first lesson in the book, with your class or group will demonstrate how a lesson is organized. The sample lesson explains how to complete the exercises and score your answers. The correct answers for the sample exercises and sample scores are printed in lighter type. In some cases, explanations of the correct answers are given. The explanations will help you understand how to think through these question types.

If you have any questions about how to complete the exercises or score them, this is the time to get the answers.

Working Through Each Lesson.   Begin each lesson by looking at the photographs and reading the captions. Before you read, predict what you think the article will be about. Then read the article.

Sometimes your teacher may decide to time your reading. Timing helps you keep track of and increase your reading speed. If you have been timed, enter your reading time in the box at the end of the lesson. Then use the Words-per-Minute Table to find your reading speed, and record your speed on the Reading Speed graph at the end of the unit.

Next complete the Reading Comprehension and Critical Thinking exercises. The directions for each exercise will tell you how to mark your answers. When you have finished all four Reading Comprehension exercises, use the answer key provided by your teacher to check your work. Follow the directions after each exercise to find your score. Record your Reading Comprehension scores on the graph at the end of each unit. Then check your answers to the Author's Approach, Summarizing and Paraphrasing, and Critical Thinking exercises. Fill in the Critical Thinking chart at the end of each unit with your evaluation of your work and comments about your progress.

At the end of each unit you will also complete a Compare/Contrast chart. The completed chart will help you see what the articles have in common, and it will give you an opportunity to explore your personal reaction to these tragic, yet spellbinding, events.

SAMPLE
LESSON

ANDREA DORIA BURIED AT SEA

The Italian luxury liner Andrea Doria *sank in the Atlantic Ocean off the coast of the United States, 45 miles south of Nantucket Island.*

It was a warm July evening in 1956. The *Andrea Doria*, after six days at sea, was nearing the end of its voyage to New York City from Genoa, Italy. The Italian liner carried a crew of 575 and 1,134 passengers. Movie stars, the mayor of Philadelphia, businessmen, and poor Italian families were among those on board the giant vessel. No other passenger ship surpassed the *Andrea Doria* in luxury.

2 In a dense fog, the *Andrea Doria* sailed at top speed toward the United States mainland, about 100 miles away. It had entered an area of the Atlantic Ocean known as "Times Square," so named because ship traffic there is usually heavy.

3 One of the ships in Times Square that night was the *Stockholm*, a sleek, modern Swedish passenger ship. The *Stockholm* had departed from New York and was bound for its home port.

4 Around 11:00 P.M. an Italian boy stood on the *Andrea Doria*'s deck, peering through the fog. He tried to catch sight of land. He knew that Nantucket, an island off the coast of Massachusetts, was out there somewhere in the pea soup fog. He strained his eyes searching through the muck. Suddenly, he thought he saw something. It took a few more seconds for him to realized what it was. He saw the enormous bulk of the *Stockholm*—and the

great edge of the white bow was heading straight for him!

5   Other people saw the *Stockholm* too. The captain and crew of the *Andrea Doria* had been watching the Swedish liner for some time on the radar screen. Captain Piero Calamai, a veteran sailor, thought that if the two ships held their course they would pass safely starboard to starboard. It wasn't until he saw the *Stockholm*'s lights that he realized the extreme danger he faced. He tried to steer his ship away from the *Stockholm*, but there wasn't enough time. The *Stockholm* started to turn to avoid a collision, then for some reason it suddenly turned again. Calamai drew back from the railing as the two ships rushed toward each other. Seconds later the *Stockholm* crashed into *Andrea Doria*'s side. The Italian liner shook from end to end and briefly lifted out of the water.

6   The *Stockholm* had a razor-sharp bow designed especially for breaking through ice. Now, that icebreaker bow sliced a V-shaped gash through the *Andrea Doria*. It finally came to a stop 30 feet inside the stricken ship. When the *Stockholm* reversed its engines and pulled back, the sea poured into the jagged, 40-foot hole in the side of the Italian ship. The *Andrea Doria* had received its death blow.

7   About 40 passengers aboard the *Andrea Doria* were killed instantly in their cabins or drowned. Walter Carlin, from Brooklyn, New York, was brushing his teeth in his cabin. The impact knocked him to the bathroom floor. Dazed and bruised, he walked back to the bedroom and found the *Stockholm*'s bow inside his cabin. His wife, who had been sleeping in her bunk, was dead. Carlin stood stunned as the ship's bow slowly moved backward. To his horror, it pulled his wife's bunk along with it. His wife's body slipped quickly into the sea.

8   Fourteen-year-old Linda Morgan was asleep in an upper bunk in cabin 52. Her younger sister slept in the lower bunk. After the collision there was nothing left of their cabin and the girls had disappeared. A crewman on the *Stockholm* found Linda, alive, lying in the wreckage. By some miracle, Linda survived being thrown from her bed and into the *Stockholm*'s bow. Her sister, however, was killed.

9   Passengers on the upper deck of the *Andrea Doria* were unaware of the chaos below. Cabins on five levels were completely destroyed. Thick smoke, twisted metal, and water filled the hallways. Fuel tanks had ruptured and were spraying oil. Severely injured people trapped under the wreckage were screaming. Others rushed to the stairways and pushed and shoved their way to the upper deck. Their clothes were wet and torn, and they were covered with oil and blood.

The Swedish liner Stockholm *rests in dry dock following its collision with the* Andrea Doria. *This photo shows how the bow was sheared in the collision.*

6

10   Aboard the *Stockholm* there was little panic and only a few casualties. The ship's bow was torn and bent like a discarded tin can, but the liner was able to stay afloat. Through the fog, passengers on the Swedish ship could hear the cries coming from the *Andrea Doria*.

11   Listing to one side, the damaged Italian ship was now in serious danger. Captain Calamai ordered the lifeboats lowered, but because of the list some boats were useless. Passengers panicked and started fighting for a place on the boats. The captain sent out an SOS. Four ships in the area answered the signal. Meanwhile, the *Stockholm* sent over its lifeboats and rescued 545 people.

12   A small freighter, the *Cape Ann*, arrived soon after the crash and picked up 129 passengers from the *Andrea Doria*. The *William H. Thomas*, steaming hard to the scene, picked up 150 victims. Another ship, the *Allen*, saved 77 people.

13   A large French liner, the *Ile de France*, was on its way to Europe when it heard the SOS. The captain radioed his message and then ordered the ship's lights turned on. The vessel had a panel of electric lights on each side of its hull that spelled out the ship's name. Passengers on the *Andrea Doria* could see the name of the French ship far in the distance and knew that more help was on the way. The *Ile de France* sailed at full speed and arrived in two hours. It rescued about 750 survivors and carried them to New York City.

14   The badly wounded *Andrea Doria* managed to stay afloat for 11 hours after the crash. That was long enough for all the survivors to be rescued. The final death count was 51.

15   Just after 10:00 in the morning, the *Andrea Doria* slipped below the ocean, bow first, and sank in 225 feet of water.

16   An investigation of the accident tried to determine if either ship had been at fault. The fog had been especially thick that July night. The *Andrea Doria* and the *Stockholm* had been in the busiest part of the Atlantic. They were headed in opposite directions in a lane used for shipping. Usually a ship stays to one side of the shipping lane. The *Stockholm* was not on the side of the lane generally used by Europe-bound ships. Both ships, however, had radar equipment in working order. How could the ships not have seen each other in plenty of time to change course? There were many theories, but nobody has ever found the answer. 🍂

If you have been timed while reading this article, enter your reading time below. Then turn to the Words-per-Minute Table on page 71 and look up your reading speed (words per minute). Enter your reading speed on the graph on page 72.

Reading Time: Sample Lesson

_____ : _____
Minutes   *Seconds*

A Finding the Main Idea

One statement below expresses the main idea of the article. One statement is too general, or too broad. The other statement explains only part of the article; it is too narrow. Label the statements using the following key:

M—Main Idea   **B—Too Broad**   **N—Too Narrow**

_____N_____ 1. The *Stockholm* cut a 40-foot hole in the *Andrea Doria*'s side. [This statement is true, but it is *too narrow*. It gives only one piece, or detail, from the story.]

_____B_____ 2. When large ships collide, there can be considerable damage. [This statement is true, but it is *too broad*. The story is about what happened to the *Andrea Doria* and the *Stockholm*.]

_____M_____ 3. The *Andrea Doria* received its death blow after colliding with the *Stockholm* in a dense fog. [This statement is the *main idea*. It tells you what the reading selection is about—two ships colliding at sea. It also tells you that there was dense fog.]

_____15_____ Score 15 points for a correct M answer.

_____10_____ Score 5 points for each correct B or N answer.

_____25_____ **Total Score:** Finding the Main Idea

B Recalling Facts

How well do you remember the facts in the article? Put an X in the box next to the answer that correctly completes each statement about the article.

1. The point in the Atlantic where the ships collided was
   ☒ a. heavily traveled.
   ☐ b. deserted because of the fog.
   ☐ c. not used by luxury liners.

2. The *Stockholm*
   ☐ a. was badly damaged by the crash.
   ☐ b. sank after the crash.
   ☒ c. crushed its bow in the crash.

3. Most of the *Andrea Doria* passengers
   ☐ a. died instantly.
   ☒ b. were rescued by the *Ile de France*.
   ☐ c. were picked up by the *Stockholm*.

4. The *Stockholm* caused so much damage to the *Andrea Doria* because it
   ☒ a. had an ice-cutter bow.
   ☐ b. was sailing at full speed.
   ☐ c. was made of very hard steel.

5. The *Andrea Doria* stayed afloat for
   ☐ a. 24 hours after the collision.
   ☐ b. 15 hours after the collision.
   ☒ c. 11 hours after the collision.

Score 5 points for each correct answer.

_____25_____ **Total Score:** Recalling Facts

C | Making Inferences

When you combine your own experience and information from a text to draw a conclusion that is not directly stated in that text, you are making an inference. Below are five statements that may or may not be inferences based on information in the article. Label the statements using the following key:

C—Correct Inference   F—Faulty Inference

___F___ 1. Passengers aboard the *Stockholm* feared that their ship would sink. [This is a *faulty* inference. There is nothing in the story to suggest that the *Stockholm* was in danger of sinking.]

___F___ 2. Captain Calamai warned his passengers to prepare for a crash. [This is a *faulty* inference. The story does not mention that the captain talked to the passengers before the crash.]

___C___ 3. The ships might have avoided a collision if it had been a clear night. [This is a *correct* inference. The story says that there was thick fog.]

___C___ 4. At first, passengers on the upper deck of the *Andrea Doria* did not think the damage was serious. [This is a *correct* inference. The passengers realized later what had happened on the decks below.]

___F___ 5. The *Stockholm* did not participate in the rescue effort. [This is a *faulty* inference. The story says that the *Stockholm* sent lifeboats over to the damaged ship.]

Score 5 points for each correct answer.

___25___ **Total Score:** Making Inferences

D | Using Words Precisely

Each numbered sentence below contains an underlined word or phrase from the article. Following the sentence are three definitions. One definition is closest to the meaning of the underlined word. One definition is opposite or nearly opposite. Label those two definitions using the following key. Do not label the remaining definition.

C—Closest   O—Opposite or Nearly Opposite

1. No other passenger ship <u>surpassed</u> the *Andrea Doria* in luxury.

   ___C___ a. was superior to

   ___O___ b. was worse than

   _____ c. named

2. Captain Piero Calamai, a <u>veteran</u> sailor, thought that if the two ships held their course they would pass safely....

   _____ a. former

   ___O___ b. unskilled

   ___C___ c. experienced

3. It [the bow] finally came to a stop 30 feet inside the <u>stricken</u> ship.

   _____ a. luxurious

   ___C___ b. damaged

   ___O___ c. untouched

4. Fuel tanks had <u>ruptured</u> and were spraying oil.

   ___C___ a. cracked

   _____ b. caught fire

   ___O___ c. repaired

5. <u>Listing</u> to one side, the damaged Italian ship was now in serious danger.

___0___ a. standing upright

___C___ b. leaning

_____ c. floating

___15___	Score 3 points for each correct C answer.
___10___	Score 2 points for each correct O answer.
___25___	**Total Score:** Using Words Precisely

Enter the four total scores in the spaces below, and add them together to find your Reading Comprehension Score. Then record your score on the graph on page 73.

Score	Question Type	Sample Lesson
___25___	Finding the Main Idea	
___25___	Recalling Facts	
___25___	Making Inferences	
___25___	Using Words Precisely	
___100___	**Reading Comprehension Score**	

Author's Approach

Put an X in the box next to the correct answer.

1. What does the author mean by the statement "He strained his eyes searching through the muck"?

☐ a. He hurt himself as he explored the garbage.

☐ b. He hurt his eyes as he explored the mess on the ship.

☒ c. He had to make an effort to see through the thick fog.

2. The main purpose of the first paragraph is to

☒ a. describe the *Andrea Doria* and its passengers.

☐ b. compare the *Andrea Doria* to less luxurious liners.

☐ c. inform the reader about transportation in the 1950s.

3. Choose the statement below that is the weakest argument for blaming the *Stockholm* for the crash.

☐ a. The *Stockholm* was not on the side of the lane generally used by Europe-bound ships.

☐ b. The *Stockholm* turned to avoid a collision, but then turned back.

☒ c. Both the *Andrea Doria* and the *Stockholm* had radar equipment in working order.

4. Choose the statement below that best describes the author's position in paragraph 13.

☐ a. The *Ile de France* took too long to come to the rescue.

☒ b. The *Ile de France* did everything it could to help survivors.

☐ c. The *Ile de France* could have done more to help survivors.

___4___	Number of correct answers

Record your personal assessment of your work on the Critical Thinking Chart on page 74.

CRITICAL THINKING

Summarizing and Paraphrasing

Put an X in the box next to the correct answer.

1. Below are summaries of the article. Choose the summary that says all the most important things about the article but in the fewest words.

☐ a. The *Stockholm* collided with the *Andrea Doria* and cut a large gash in the ship.

☐ b. When the *Stockholm* sliced through the *Andrea Doria*, about 40 passengers on board the ship were killed instantly. Several ships in the area, including the *Stockholm*, the *Cape Ann*, the *William H. Thomas*, the *Allen*, and the *Ile de France*, came to the *Andrea Doria*'s rescue. The final death count in the crash was 51. No one has ever been able to explain why the ships collided.

☒ c. The *Stockholm* collided with the *Andrea Doria*, cutting a large gash in the ship. In all, 51 people died in the crash; the survivors were rescued by several ships in the area. Although the fog was thick at the time of the crash, no one has been able to explain why the ships crashed.

2. Choose the sentence that correctly restates the following sentence from the article:

"[The *Andrea Doria*] had entered an area of the Atlantic Ocean known as 'Times Square,' so named because ship traffic there is usually heavy."

☒ a. The *Andrea Doria* sailed into a heavily traveled part of the Atlantic called Times Square.

☐ b. The *Andrea Doria* entered the Atlantic Ocean, which is also called Times Square.

☐ c. The *Andrea Doria* sailed past Times Square, a crowded part of New York City.

___2___ Number of correct answers

Record your personal assessment of your work on the Critical Thinking Chart on page 74.

Critical Thinking

Put an X in the box next to the correct answer for questions 1, 3, and 4. Follow the directions provided for the other question.

1. From what the article told about where the *Andrea Doria* received its death blow, you can conclude that

☐ a. people in the cabins had a better chance of survival.

☒ b. people on the upper deck had a better chance of survival.

☐ c. the captain had the least chance of survival.

2. Choose from the letters below to correctly complete the following statement. Write the letters on the lines.

In the article, _____*b*_____ and _____*c*_____ are alike.

a. Mrs. Carlin's fate

b. Linda Morgan's fate

c. Walter Carlin's fate

3. What was the effect of the *Andrea Doria*'s listing to one side?

☒ a. Some of the lifeboats were useless.

☐ b. The ship's bow was bent like an old tin can.

☐ c. The ship sank immediately.

4. What did you have to do to answer question 2?

☐ a. find an effect (something that happened)

☐ b. find a definition (what something means)

☒ c. find a comparison (how things are the same)

_____5_____ Number of correct answers

Record your personal assessment of your work on the Critical Thinking Chart on page 74.

Personal Response

What new question do you have about this topic?

[Write down a question that came to mind as you read the article.]

Self-Assessment

While reading the article, I found it easiest to

[Tell what you had the least trouble with as you read the article.]

CRITICAL THINKING

Self-Assessment

To get the most out of the Critical Reading series program, you need to take charge of your own progress in improving your reading comprehension and critical thinking skills. Here are some of the features that help you work on those essential skills.

Reading Comprehension Exercises. Complete these exercises immediately after reading the article. They help you recall what you have read, understand the stated and implied main ideas, and add words to your working vocabulary.

Critical Thinking Skills Exercises. These exercises help you focus on the author's approach and purpose, recognize and generate summaries and paraphrases, and identify relationships between ideas.

Personal Response and Self-assessment. Questions in this category help you relate the articles to your personal experience and give you the opportunity to evaluate your understanding of the information in that lesson.

Compare and Contrast Charts. At the end of each unit you will complete a Compare and Contrast chart. The completed chart helps you see what the articles have in common and gives you an opportunity to explore your own ideas about the topics discussed in the articles.

The Graphs. The graphs and charts at the end of each unit enable you to keep track of your progress. Check your graphs regularly with your teacher. Decide whether your progress is satisfactory or whether you need additional work on some skills. What types of exercises are you having difficulty with? Talk with your teacher about ways to work on the skills in which you need the most practice.

UNIT ONE

DEATH OF A DREAM

Eighteen members of the U.S. figure skating team (with their manager at left) are photographed on Valentine's Day, 1961 before leaving the United States for competition in Prague, Czechoslovakia.

They boarded the plane in New York City with high hopes. The 18 members of the United States figure skating team would fly to Brussels, Belgium. Then they were to go on to Prague, Czechoslovakia, for the world ice skating championships. A photo was taken of the team members as they stood on the steps of the Sabena Airlines 707 jet. The best of America's skaters beamed for the camera. Mostly young, they laughed and giggled, their eyes dancing with excitement. This was going to be the time of their lives.

2 There were three ice skating pairs on the plane. Two were brother-and-sister teams: Laurie and William Hickox and Ida and Ray Hadley. There was also the husband-and-wife team of Patricia and Robert Dineen. But the brightest star of all was a singles skater. Her name was Laurence "Laurie" Owen. Only 16 years old, she had won the North American title for women just two days earlier. Laurie had great skill, dazzling grace, and a winning smile. *Sports Illustrated* reported

that "Her free skating has an air, a style, an individuality which sets it apart...." Laurie was America's top candidate to capture a gold medal at the 1964 Olympics.

3   Laurie came from a skating family. Her mother, Maribel, had won the U.S. figure skating championship nine times. Now, at the age of 49, she was one of the nation's top coaches. One of her students, Tenley Albright, had won the Olympic gold medal in 1956. After Laurie had won the North American title, Maribel was asked if she had felt like she was in the rink with her daughter. "You bet," she said. "I skated every stroke with her."

4   Laurie had an older sister who shared her mother's name. Maribel Owen, age 20, was not quite as strong a skater as Laurie. Still, she had just won the U.S. senior pairs championship. All three of the Owen women were on the plane bound for Brussels.

5   Sabena Flight 548 took off at 7:30 P.M. on February 14, 1961. The flight across the Atlantic was pleasant. Early the next day, the plane neared the airport at Brussels. There seemed to be no cause for concern. There was no distress signal of any kind from the pilot, Captain Louis Lambrechts. There were no storms or high winds in the region. In fact, the weather was perfect. It was warm and sunny.

6   But something must have gone wrong in the cockpit. During the last few minutes before the scheduled landing, Captain Lambrechts did not contact the Brussels airport. Just before 10 A.M., he lowered the wheels of the jet and began his approach to land. But at the last moment, he pulled the plane up. Perhaps he saw another jet taking off and feared a collision. Or perhaps he already knew that something was wrong with his plane. In any case, he circled the airport and prepared to try again.

Firefighters and rescue workers pick through the charred wreckage of the Sabena jet in a field near the Brussels airport on February 15, 1961.

7   Lambrechts came in a second time, flying about 500 feet over a farm near the village of Berg, northeast of Brussels. Then he suddenly increased his speed and pulled the plane into a steep climb. By this time, officials in the Brussels control tower could tell that something was very wrong. "We saw the crash coming," said one official. "It looked as if the plane's controls had been lost completely." Fire trucks and ambulances were ordered to go to the area even before the plane crashed. "They couldn't have been faster," the official said. "But there was nothing they could do."

8   A woman in Berg saw the whole thing. "I could see people looking at me from inside the plane and gesturing…. Then the plane stopped right in the air," she said. "The whole thing was shaking terribly, as if it were struggling to get started moving again. But something was holding it back. The plane began to point to the sky. The whole nose began to rise upward."

9   A man riding on a train also saw that the plane was in trouble. "The plane appeared to be making a normal approach to land when it suddenly reared up into the sky," he said. "Then it fell back like a great stone and we heard the explosion."

10   It was 10:05 A.M. when the Sabena jet hit the ground and exploded in a ball of flames. It just missed hitting a row of houses. All 72 people on board were killed, including 49 Americans and 11 members of the crew. There was nothing anyone could do. The crash site was a scene of total destruction. Debris was scattered over 200 yards. Charred remains and body parts were strewn all over the area. Several couples on the plane were found locked in a final embrace.

11   A young farmer who had been tilling his cabbage patch was killed when the plane crashed into his field. A piece of flying debris severed the leg of another man on the ground. Luckily, a rescuer managed to apply a tourniquet to keep this man from bleeding to death.

12   The crash stunned skaters and figure skating fans around the globe. Never before had anything so tragic happened in their sport. To honor the dead, the Prague competition was canceled. The crash was particularly devastating for some families. In addition to the Owen family with its loss of three women, nine other skating families suffered more than one death. The hopes and dreams of these athletes had ended in a flash. All that remained as rescuers combed through the wreckage were three pairs of melted skates dangling from one of the wings.

If you have been timed while reading this article, enter your reading time below. Then turn to the Words-per-Minute Table on page 71 and look up your reading speed (words per minute). Enter your reading speed on the graph on page 72.

Reading Time: Lesson 1

_____ : _____
Minutes   Seconds

A | Finding the Main Idea

One statement below expresses the main idea of the article. One statement is too general, or too broad. The other statement explains only part of the article; it is too narrow. Label the statements using the following key:

M—Main Idea   B—Too Broad   N—Too Narrow

_____ 1. The crash of Sabena Flight 548 was a great tragedy for the sport of figure skating.

_____ 2. Skater Laurie Owen, who was killed in the plane crash, had won the North American singles title just two days earlier.

_____ 3. In February 1961, Sabena Flight 548 crashed killing everyone on board, including 18 members of the U.S. figure skating team.

_____ Score 15 points for a correct M answer.

_____ Score 5 points for each correct B or N answer.

_____ **Total Score:** Finding the Main Idea

B | Recalling Facts

How well do you remember the facts in the article? Put an X in the box next to the answer that correctly completes each statement about the article.

1. Eighteen members of the United States figure skating team were on their way to the world ice skating championships in
   ☐ a. Brussels, Belgium.
   ☐ b. Prague, Czechoslovakia.
   ☐ c. Berg, Belgium.

2. The brightest star on the skating team at that time was
   ☐ a. Maribel Owen.
   ☐ b. Tenley Albright.
   ☐ c. Laurie Owen.

3. Sabena Flight 548 was making its first approach to land when
   ☐ a. Captain Lambrechts pulled the plane up and circled the airport.
   ☐ b. the plane collided with another jet.
   ☐ c. the plane crashed on a farm in Berg.

4. Before the crash, officials in the Brussels control tower
   ☐ a. had no idea anything was wrong.
   ☐ b. knew that something was very wrong with the plane.
   ☐ c. did not bother sending fire trucks and ambulances to the area.

5. To honor the dead skaters, the world ice skating competition
   ☐ a. was canceled.
   ☐ b. went on as scheduled.
   ☐ c. was dedicated to the American athletes.

Score 5 points for each correct answer.

_____ **Total Score:** Recalling Facts

C | Making Inferences

When you combine your own experience and information from a text to draw a conclusion that is not directly stated in that text, you are making an inference. Below are five statements that may or may not be inferences based on information in the article. Label the statements using the following key:

C—Correct Inference   F—Faulty Inference

_____ 1. Even before the plane made its first approach, Captain Lambrechts knew something was wrong with the 707 jet.

_____ 2. Weather conditions had nothing to do with the crash of the Sabena flight.

_____ 3. Seconds before the impact, passengers on board had no idea that their plane was about to crash.

_____ 4. Officials in the Brussels control tower acted quickly in the emergency.

_____ 5. More people would have been killed if the plane had not missed hitting a row of houses.

Score 5 points for each correct answer.

_____ **Total Score:** Making Inferences

D | Using Words Precisely

Each numbered sentence below contains an underlined word or phrase from the article. Following the sentence are three definitions. One definition is closest to the meaning of the underlined word. One definition is opposite or nearly opposite. Label those two definitions using the following key. Do not label the remaining definition.

C—Closest   O—Opposite or Nearly Opposite

1. The best of America's skaters <u>beamed</u> for the camera.

_____ a. waved

_____ b. smiled

_____ c. frowned

2. Laurie had great skill, <u>dazzling</u> grace, and a winning smile.

_____ a. common

_____ b. sharp

_____ c. amazing

3. *Sports Illustrated* reported that "Her free skating has an air, a style, an <u>individuality</u> which sets it apart...."

_____ a. quality of being unique and different

_____ b. ordinariness

_____ c. fearlessness

4. Perhaps he saw another jet taking off and feared a <u>collision</u>.

_____ a. near miss

_____ b. crash

_____ c. competition

5. Charred remains and body parts were <u>strewn</u> all over the area.

_____ a. hidden

_____ b. collected

_____ c. scattered

_____ Score 3 points for each correct C answer.

_____ Score 2 points for each correct O answer.

_____ **Total Score:** Using Words Precisely

Enter the four total scores in the spaces below, and add them together to find your Reading Comprehension Score. Then record your score on the graph on page 73.

Score	Question Type	Lesson 1
_____	Finding the Main Idea	
_____	Recalling Facts	
_____	Making Inferences	
_____	Using Words Precisely	
_____	**Reading Comprehension Score**	

Author's Approach

Put an X in the box next to the correct answer.

1. What does the author mean by the statement "This was going to be the time of their lives"?

☐ a. The skaters were nervous about the ice skating competition.

☐ b. The skaters were looking forward to having a wonderful time.

☐ c. The American skaters were favored to win the championship.

2. The main purpose of the first paragraph is to

☐ a. describe the excitement of the figure skating team.

☐ b. compare the American figure skating team to European teams.

☐ c. inform the reader about the world ice skating championships.

3. What is the author's purpose in writing "Death of a Dream"?

☐ a. To express an opinion about Captain Lambrechts's ability as a pilot

☐ b. To inform the reader about a plane crash that killed many members of the U.S. figure skating team

☐ c. To convey a mood of excitement

4. Which of the following statements from the article best describes Laurie Owen's skating style?

☐ a. "Laurie came from a skating family."

☐ b. "Laurie had an older sister who shared her mother's name."

☐ c. "Laurie had great skill, dazzling grace, and a winning smile."

_____ Number of correct answers

Record your personal assessment of your work on the Critical Thinking Chart on page 74.

Summarizing and Paraphrasing

Follow the directions provided for questions 1 and 2. Put an X in the box next to the correct answer for question 3.

1. Look for the important ideas and events in paragraphs 3 and 4. Summarize those paragraphs in one or two sentences.

_____

_____

_____

2. Reread paragraph 10 in the article. Below, write a summary of the paragraph in no more than 25 words.

_____

_____

_____

_____

_____

Reread your summary and decide whether it covers the important ideas in the paragraph. Next, decide how to shorten the summary to 15 words or less without leaving out any essential information. Write this summary below.

_____

_____

_____

3. Read the statement about the article below. Then read the paraphrase of that statement. Choose the reason that best tells why the paraphrase does not say the same thing as the statement.

Statement: The plane crash was particularly devastating for the Owens and nine other skating families, each of which suffered more than one death.

Paraphrase: The Owens were the only skaters to lose more than one family member in the plane crash.

☐ a.   Paraphrase says too much.

☐ b.   Paraphrase doesn't say enough.

☐ c.   Paraphrase doesn't agree with the statement about the article.

_____ Number of correct answers

Record your personal assessment of your work on the Critical Thinking Chart on page 74.

Critical Thinking

Put an X in the box next to the correct answer for questions 1 and 4. Follow the directions provided for the other questions.

1. From the article, you can predict that if the plane hadn't crashed,

☐ a.   Laurie Owen would have continued to win skating titles and championships.

☐ b.   Laurie's sister Maribel would have won the gold medal at the 1964 Olympics.

☐ c.   Laurie's mother Maribel would have quit coaching.

CRITICAL THINKING

2. Choose from the letters below to correctly complete the following statement. Write the letters on the lines.

In the article, _____ and _____ are alike.

a. the relationship between Laurie and William Hickox

b. the relationship between Patricia and Robert Dineen

c. the relationship between Ida and Ray Hadley

3. Read paragraph 11. Then choose from the letters below to correctly complete the following statement. Write the letters on the lines.

According to paragraph 11, _____ because _____.

a. a rescuer used a tourniquet to stop his bleeding

b. a young farmer was killed by the airplane

c. a man's life was saved

4. What did you have to do to answer question 2?

☐ a. find a cause (why something happened)

☐ b. find a comparison (how things are the same)

☐ c. draw a conclusion (a sensible statement based on the text and your experience)

_____ Number of correct answers

Record your personal assessment of your work on the Critical Thinking Chart on page 74.

Personal Response

Would you recommend this article to other students? Explain.

_____

_____

_____

_____

Self-Assessment

A word or phrase in the article that I do not understand is

_____

_____

_____

CRITICAL THINKING

CUSTER'S LAST STAND
Battle of the Little Bighorn

The hot June sun glared down on Lieutenant Colonel Custer and his 225 weary soldiers. Time was running out, and Custer knew their only chance to survive was to charge the hill in front of them. Behind them, Chief Gall and 1,500 warriors were already attacking.

2   Custer may have paused to glance up at the crest of the hill. If he did, he would have seen that Crazy Horse and at least 1,000 warriors had reached the crest before him. The Sioux and Cheyenne had the Seventh Cavalry surrounded.

3   As the smoke from the guns and the clouds of churning dust cleared, only a few white men remained standing. Dead and dying men and horses covered the slope near the Little Bighorn River. Custer was one of the few troopers still on his feet. But in 20 minutes or less, the battle would be over. Custer and every soldier with him would be dead.

* * *

4   Probably no other battle in the history of the United States has caused more controversy than the Battle of the Little

This picture shows Chief Crazy Horse (center, in spotted war paint) at the Battle of the Little Big Horn on June 25, 1876. It was painted by Amos Bad Heart Bull, an Oglala Sioux from the Pine Ridge Reservation.

Bighorn. Why did Custer suffer such a crushing defeat?

5   George Armstrong Custer always wanted to be a soldier. In 1861 he graduated last in his class from West Point. But during the Civil War he quickly proved that he was a fearless leader. By the age of 25 he was made a major general.

6   Many who served with the "boy general" in the war thought he was a brave man. Yet many others felt he was a proud, overbearing "glory hunter." They resented his flashy style. Instead of the army uniform, he sometimes wore a fringed buckskin suit. And he often disobeyed orders.

7   But now the Civil War was over and the army didn't need as many generals. Custer was cut in rank to lieutenant colonel. He was assigned second-in-command of the newly formed Seventh Cavalry.

8   The main tasks of the army were to protect the crews building the railroads in the West and to deal with the Plains Indians. In 1874 Custer marched into the Black Hills for an exploratory trip. After surveying the area, Custer sent a scout back to the fort with a news release: Gold in the Black Hills! But years earlier, a treaty had given that land to the Sioux. No white person could use the land without the permission of the Sioux.

9   The desire for gold proved too strong to resist. In less than a year, thousands of miners and their families poured into the region. The government wanted the Sioux to sell their land.

10   The Sioux refused to sell. They banded together with the Cheyenne near the Little Bighorn River. In their camp of

General George Armstrong Custer photographed by the well-known Civil War photographer Matthew Brady

thousands of men, women, and children there were at least 3,000 warriors.

11 Custer was eager to battle the Sioux and Cheyenne. He felt that a victory was the only way to restore his reputation with President Ulysses S. Grant. Custer had served under Grant during the war. But recently Custer had angered the president. Grant's brother had been involved in a scandal, and Custer had testified against him. An enraged Grant took away Custer's command.

12 At last Custer's friend, Major General Alfred Terry, persuaded Grant to let Custer return to the Seventh Cavalry and Fort Abraham Lincoln in what is now North Dakota. Grant agreed, but insisted that Terry be in command. Custer and the Seventh were now part of Terry's force. Their job was to find the Sioux-Cheyenne camp.

13 In June 1876 Terry's forces were to meet up with those of Colonel Gibbon and General Crook. But Crook's forces were attacked along the way and unable to join Terry. Terry gave Custer orders to lead the Seventh to the Little Bighorn valley and *wait* for Terry and the others to join him.

14 Custer wanted to make sure that he won the glory of defeating the Plains Indians. He and the Seventh made a forced march to the Little Bighorn River. For days they rode late into the night and started again before dawn. Custer arrived at the meeting place well before schedule.

15 Even though Terry had ordered Custer to do nothing until the others arrived, Custer had no intention of waiting. His

scouts warned him that the Sioux camp they found was larger than any they'd ever seen before. Still, Custer ignored their warnings and decided to attack.

16 Then Custer made another devastating mistake. He divided his already outnumbered Seventh. He told Captain Frederick Benteen to take 125 men and sweep south of the river valley. Major Marcus Reno was given 140 men and told by Custer, "Take your battalion and try to bring them to battle, and I will support you with the whole outfit."

17 Why did Custer divide his troops? Did he realize what he was asking of Reno? He was sending Reno to attack the south end of what was probably the largest group of Plains Indians ever to assemble.

18 Custer and his 225 men galloped into the ravine toward the Indian camp. In the meantime, Reno was under attack and waiting for Custer to join him. Reno was a capable officer, but neither he nor his tired men had any experience fighting the Indians. The warriors outnumbered the soldiers and had better weapons. The soldiers carried single-shot rifles. The Indians had the latest Winchester repeaters.

19 After 20 minutes of fighting, Reno ordered a retreat. Benteen met up with Reno. Neither command could reach Custer because they were driven back by the Sioux.

20 Custer and his men were trapped. And they were outnumbered by more than 10 to 1. Most of the troopers' rifles jammed, which meant the soldiers had to use

knives to dig the cases from the chambers and then reload. The Indians kept up a steady stream of weapon fire. As the ranks of soldiers thinned, the Sioux and Cheyenne moved in and killed the remaining troops with knives and hatchets. The Sioux and Cheyenne attack, directed by Sitting Bull, Crazy Horse, and Gall, ended when Custer and all 225 men were dead. The only survivor was a horse named Comanche. After the attack, the Seventh made sure that the badly wounded Comanche was returned to the fort. He became a symbol of the Battle at Little Bighorn.

21 Many feel that Custer lost the now-famous battle but won the war. Soon after his defeat, the Plains Indians were forced to sell their land and move onto reservations 🌿

If you have been timed while reading this article, enter your reading time below. Then turn to the Words-per-Minute Table on page 71 and look up your reading speed (words per minute). Enter your reading speed on the graph on page 72.

Reading Time: Lesson 2

_____ : _____
Minutes   Seconds

A | Finding the Main Idea

One statement below expresses the main idea of the article. One statement is too general, or too broad. The other statement explains only part of the article; it is too narrow. Label the statements using the following key:

M—Main Idea   **B—Too Broad**   **N—Too Narrow**

_____ 1. In 1876, Custer and the 225 men of the Seventh Cavalry were wiped out completely by a Sioux-Cheyenne force near the Little Bighorn River.

_____ 2. Custer and his defeat have been a subject of interest to historians for years.

_____ 3. At least 3,000 Sioux and Cheyenne warriors were camped at Little Bighorn.

_____ Score 15 points for a correct M answer.

_____ Score 5 points for each correct B or N answer.

_____ **Total Score:** Finding the Main Idea

B | Recalling Facts

How well do you remember the facts in the article? Put an X in the box next to the answer that correctly completes each statement about the article.

1. Custer had fought in the
   - ☐ a. Civil War.
   - ☐ b. Mexican War.
   - ☐ c. American Revolution.

2. Custer's cavalry included Captain Benteen and
   - ☐ a. Colonel Gibbon.
   - ☐ b. Major Marcus Reno.
   - ☐ c. Major General Alfred Terry.

3. When Reno's command began to lose the fight, they
   - ☐ a. went back to the fort.
   - ☐ b. retreated.
   - ☐ c. surrendered.

4. The Battle of the Little Bighorn occurred in
   - ☐ a. September 1875.
   - ☐ b. May 1861.
   - ☐ c. June 1876.

5. The Seventh Cavalry was equipped with
   - ☐ a. single-shot rifles.
   - ☐ b. Winchester repeaters.
   - ☐ c. knives.

Score 5 points for each correct answer.

_____ **Total Score:** Recalling Facts

C Making Inferences

When you combine your own experience and information from a text to draw a conclusion that is not directly stated in that text, you are making an inference. Below are five statements that may or may not be inferences based on information in the article. Label the statements using the following key:

C—Correct Inference   F—Faulty Inference

_____ 1. Custer will not be remembered for his skilled leadership.

_____ 2. The Seventh Cavalry used old rifles and ammunition.

_____ 3. Major General Terry disliked Custer.

_____ 4. The Sioux and Cheyenne cared more about the gold than their land.

_____ 5. Everyone was surprised that Custer disobeyed General Terry's orders.

Score 5 points for each correct answer.

_____ **Total Score:** Making Inferences

D Using Words Precisely

Each numbered sentence below contains an underlined word or phrase from the article. Following the sentence are three definitions. One definition is closest to the meaning of the underlined word. One definition is opposite or nearly opposite. Label those two definitions using the following key. Do not label the remaining definition.

C—Closest   O—Opposite or Nearly Opposite

1. Yet many others felt he was a proud, <u>overbearing</u>, a "glory hunter."

_____ a. bossy

_____ b. meek

_____ c. intelligent

2. They <u>resented</u> his flashy style.

_____ a. were frightened by

_____ b. were offended by

_____ c. were delighted by

3. In 1874 Custer marched into the Black Hills for an <u>exploratory</u> trip.

_____ a. useless

_____ b. fact-finding

_____ c. short

4. He felt that a victory was the only way to <u>restore</u> his reputation with President Ulysses S. Grant.

_____ a. rebuild

_____ b. discuss

_____ c. destroy

5. Then Custer made another <u>devastating</u> mistake.

_____ a. unusual

_____ b. helpful

_____ c. disastrous

_____ Score 3 points for each correct C answer.

_____ Score 2 points for each correct O answer.

_____ **Total Score:** Using Words Precisely

Enter the four total scores in the spaces below, and add them together to find your Reading Comprehension Score. Then record your score on the graph on page 73.

Score	Question Type	Lesson 2
_____	Finding the Main Idea	
_____	Recalling Facts	
_____	Making Inferences	
_____	Using Words Precisely	
_____	**Reading Comprehension Score**	

Author's Approach

Put an X in the box next to the correct answer.

1. Which of the following statements from the article best describes Custer's personality?

☐ a. "George Armstrong Custer always wanted to be a soldier."

☐ b. "In 1861 he graduated last in his class from West Point."

☐ c. "Yet many others felt he was a proud, overbearing, 'glory hunter.'"

2. What does the author imply by saying "Many feel that Custer lost the now-famous battle but won the war"?

☐ a. Although Custer and his men were overcome in this fight, their opponents were eventually defeated by the U.S. forces.

☐ b. The other forces from the Seventh Cavalry managed to defeat the Indians at Little Bighorn.

☐ c. Custer won other battles that led to the defeat of the Indians.

3. The author probably wrote this article in order to

☐ a. express a negative opinion of Custer.

☐ b. compare Custer's soldiers to the Indian warriors.

☐ c. tell the reader about Custer and the Battle of the Little Bighorn.

CRITICAL THINKING

4. How is the author's purpose for writing the article expressed in paragraph 15?

☐ a. The author tells the reader that a great many Sioux were prepared to fight at Little Bighorn.

☐ b. The author suggests that Custer had no concern for his tired troops.

☐ c. The author tells the reader about some of the mistakes Custer made in preparing for the battle.

_____ Number of correct answers

Record your personal assessment of your work on the Critical Thinking Chart on page 74.

Summarizing and Paraphrasing

Put an X in the box next to the correct answer.

1. Below are summaries of the article. Choose the summary that says all the most important things about the article but in the fewest words.

☐ a. Custer lost the Battle of the Little Bighorn. Custer and all of his men were killed in the battle.

☐ b. Eager to defeat the Sioux and Cheyenne at the Battle of the Little Bighorn, Custer made a series of mistakes that led to his defeat. Custer and all of his men were killed.

☐ c. Custer wanted to fight the Sioux and Cheyenne at the Battle of the Little Bighorn because he wanted to restore his reputation with President Grant. However, after Custer divided his troops, he was hopelessly outnumbered by the strong Indian force. Custer and all 225 of his men were killed in the battle.

2. Choose the sentence that correctly restates the following sentence from the article:

"Most of the troopers' rifles jammed, which meant the soldiers had to use knives to dig the cases from the chambers and then reload."

☐ a. Because their rifles jammed, most of the soldiers had to use knives to fight the Indians while they reloaded.

☐ b. Before they could reload, the soldiers had to use knives to unjam their rifles.

☐ c. Before they could reload their rifles, the soldiers had to use knives to dig their ammunition out of the ground.

_____ Number of correct answers

Record your personal assessment of your work on the Critical Thinking Chart on page 74.

Critical Thinking

Put an X in the box next to the correct answer for questions 1, 2, 3, and 4. Follow the directions provided for question 5.

1. Which of the following statements from the article is an opinion rather than a fact?

☐ a. "[N]o other battle in the history of the United States has caused more controversy than the Battle of the Little Bighorn."

☐ b. "By the age of 23 he [Custer] was made a brigadier general."

☐ c. "The only survivor from Custer's command was a horse named Comanche."

2. From what the article told about the U.S. government's treatment of the Sioux, you can predict that

☐ a. the government respected the wishes of all Native Americans.

☐ b. all Native Americans came to trust the government.

☐ c. the government valued the wishes of U.S. citizens over those of Native Americans.

3. What was the cause of Custer's being cut in rank to lieutenant colonel?

☐ a. After the Civil War, the army was smaller and didn't need as many generals.

☐ b. Custer had angered President Grant.

☐ c. Custer lost the Battle of the Little Bighorn.

4. Of the following theme categories, which would this story fit into?

☐ a. The desire for wealth is the root of all evil.

☐ b. Too much pride can lead to a downfall.

☐ c. Violence is not an effective way to settle differences.

5. In which paragraph did you find the information or details to answer question 3?

_____

_____ Number of correct answers

Record your personal assessment of your work on the Critical Thinking Chart on page 74.

Personal Response

Why do you think Custer disobeyed his orders and decided to attack the Indians without waiting for the other forces?

_____

_____

_____

_____

Self-Assessment

I'm proud of how I answered question # _____ in section _____ because

_____

_____

_____

_____

CRITICAL THINKING

TRAGEDY AT THE SUNSHINE SILVER MINE

Ron Flory embraces his wife after he and fellow miner Tom Wilkenson were rescued from the Sunshine Silver Mine in Kellogg, Idaho, on May 9, 1972.

Sometimes what seems bad at first actually turns out to be good. Chuck Carver found that out on May 2, 1972. Carver should have been working 3,700 feet below the ground that day. His job was with the Sunshine Silver Mine in Kellogg, Idaho. The 12-year veteran miner should have been driving the train that hauls timber and supplies through the underground shafts. But Carver had been injured a few weeks earlier. He hadn't recovered enough to return to work. That accident turned out to be a lucky break for Carver. In fact, it saved his life. On May 2, at 11 A.M., a deadly flash fire broke out in the mine not far from where Carver would have been working.

2   The Sunshine Silver Mine, the deepest and richest silver mine in the country, had a fine safety record. The mine was discovered in 1884. Since then, there had been just one fire. That was in 1946, and no one had been hurt. The record was especially impressive given the huge size of the mine. One mining official compared it to "a big apartment house with many, many rooms." It was nearly one mile deep and had more than one hundred miles of shafts and tunnels.

3   Over the years, the people of Kellogg had gotten used to thinking of their mine

as safe. The Sunshine Silver Mine didn't seem like the mines with poor safety records. As one woman said after the May 2nd fire, "It just doesn't seem real, does it? You read about it in other places, but it never happens here."

4   Still, it was a mine. And mining has always been a notoriously hard, dirty, and dangerous line of work. Temperatures in the Sunshine Silver Mine often exceeded 100 degrees. Fresh air had to be pumped in through special shafts. Cave-ins and flash fires were always a threat because many of the tunnels were braced by old wooden timbers. In the back of their minds, the miners knew the risks. But that didn't stop them from doing their jobs. They worked in the mine mostly because the pay and the benefits were good. "We all understand the danger," said Chuck Carver. "That's something everyone knows. We just don't talk too much about it.... Besides, someone's got to do it; it's my job."

5   The fire started at the 3,700-foot level. It began in a part of the mine that was blocked off and no longer in use. Apparently, the fire burned for some time before anyone noticed it. At last, however, the searing heat and expanding gases built up until they blew out the retaining bulkhead.

6   The fire then quickly spread along the open shafts and tunnels. Miners working above the fire were able to escape without much trouble. Unfortunately, those working below the fire were trapped. Dozens of miners perished in the blaze. Many died within a short time. It wasn't the flames that killed them. It was the lethal smoke and gas created by the fire. A person can breathe such poisonous fumes for only a minute or so before blacking out. A few miners, it seemed, never saw the smoke and gas coming. Rescuers found them slumped over their coffee cups.

7   Trying to rescue miners who might still be alive proved to be a daunting task. The rescuers faced all sorts of problems. These ranged from power failures to faulty ventilation equipment. Still, the rescuers kept at it day after day after day. Anxious relatives and friends waited nervously at the mine's entrance. For seven long days, the rescuers tried one scheme after another. They desperately wanted to save any miners who might still be alive. But for a time, all they found were dead bodies.

8   Then on the eighth day, they got lucky. They found two men still alive. Ron Flory and Tom Wilkenson had all but given up hope of ever being found. Then

they heard voices and saw lights in the rough and dark tunnel. "I thought we were seeing things, but we began beating on the pipes," said Flory. "It was great, just great."

A rescue crew heads into the Sunshine Silver Mine on May 7, 1972, five days after the fire started.

9   How did they survive? Flory, Wilkenson, and seven other men were at the 4,800-foot level when they noticed the smoke. The men all raced down a horizontal tunnel toward an air shaft. It was a close race with death. Flory and Wilkenson, who led the way, made it. The others weren't quite fast enough to outrun the smoke. "They were headed out, but they just didn't make it," said Flory.

10   Flory and Wilkenson survived 175 hours at the bottom of the mine. The fumes soon began to clear out because of the mine's ventilation system. Luckily the fire had started in the morning. The two men were able to eat the lunches and drink from the thermos bottles of the seven dead men. They also tapped water from a water line they found in the air shaft. Flory and Wilkenson cheered each other up whenever one of them got depressed. To pass the time, they braided blasting wire. "You have to have something to do with your hands or you'd go out of your mind," said Wilkenson. "We talked a lot, prayed a lot. We knew that between us we'd be able to stand it."

11   Although the rescuers continued to look for other survivors, they found none.

Ninety-one men died in the Sunshine Silver Mine—including Roberto Diaz, the man who replaced Chuck Carver. The fire was the worst mining disaster in the history of Idaho and one of the worst in American history. The mine owners gave Flory and Wilkenson each a $1,000 bonus for their ordeal. But Ron Flory wasn't going to risk being trapped once more. "I'll never go underground again," he said. 🍃

If you have been timed while reading this article, enter your reading time below. Then turn to the Words-per-Minute Table on page 71 and look up your reading speed (words per minute). Enter your reading speed on the graph on page 72.

Reading Time: Lesson 3

_____ : _____
Minutes   Seconds

A | Finding the Main Idea

One statement below expresses the main idea of the article. One statement is too general, or too broad. The other statement explains only part of the article; it is too narrow. Label the statements using the following key:

M—Main Idea   **B—Too Broad**   **N—Too Narrow**

_____ 1. Because Chuck Carver had been injured, he did not work in the Sunshine Silver Mine on the day of the fire.

_____ 2. A fire in the Sunshine Silver Mine killed 91 people, making it the worst mining disaster in the history of Idaho.

_____ 3. Mining is a very dangerous job.

_____ Score 15 points for a correct M answer.

_____ Score 5 points for each correct B or N answer.

_____ **Total Score:** Finding the Main Idea

B | Recalling Facts

How well do you remember the facts in the article? Put an X in the box next to the answer that correctly completes each statement about the article.

1. The Sunshine Silver Mine was discovered in
   - ☐ a. 1972.
   - ☐ b. 1946.
   - ☐ c. 1884.

2. Most men worked in the Sunshine Silver Mine because
   - ☐ a. the pay and the benefits were good.
   - ☐ b. they didn't realize that mining was such a dangerous job.
   - ☐ c. fresh air was pumped into the mine through special shafts.

3. Many of those who died in the Sunshine Silver Mine were killed by
   - ☐ a. the fire's flames.
   - ☐ b. the smoke and gas created by the fire.
   - ☐ c. collapsing tunnels.

4. When they noticed the smoke, Flory and Wilkenson
   - ☐ a. began beating on the pipes.
   - ☐ b. began to pray.
   - ☐ c. raced toward an air shaft.

5. To pass the time until they were rescued, Flory and Wilkenson
   - ☐ a. braided blasting wire.
   - ☐ b. looked for other survivors.
   - ☐ c. ran races.

Score 5 points for each correct answer.

_____ **Total Score:** Recalling Facts

C Making Inferences

When you combine your own experience and information from a text to draw a conclusion that is not directly stated in that text, you are making an inference. Below are five statements that may or may not be inferences based on information in the article. Label the statements using the following key:

C—Correct Inference   F—Faulty Inference

_____ 1. Ron Flory quit his mining job shortly after he was rescued.

_____ 2. Chuck Carver would have died if he had gone to work in the Sunshine Silver Mine on May 2.

_____ 3. The rescuers were overjoyed when they found that Flory and Wilkenson were still alive.

_____ 4. Flory and Wilkenson fought over food and water while they were trapped underground.

_____ 5. After the first day, no one believed that any miners had survived the fire.

Score 5 points for each correct answer.

_____ **Total Score:** Making Inferences

D Using Words Precisely

Each numbered sentence below contains an underlined word or phrase from the article. Following the sentence are three definitions. One definition is closest to the meaning of the underlined word. One definition is opposite or nearly opposite. Label those two definitions using the following key. Do not label the remaining definition.

C—Closest   O—Opposite or Nearly Opposite

1. And mining has always been a <u>notoriously</u> hard, dirty, and dangerous line of work.

_____ a. disgracefully

_____ b. honorably

_____ c. unusually

2. The record was especially <u>impressive</u> given the huge size of the mine.

_____ a. boring

_____ b. crowded

_____ c. remarkable and awe-inspiring

3. It was the <u>lethal</u> smoke and gas created by the fire.

_____ a. thick

_____ b. deadly

_____ c. harmless

4. Trying to rescue miners who might still be alive proved to be a <u>daunting</u> task.

_____ a. encouraging

_____ b. frustrating

_____ c. popular

5. The mine owners gave Flory and Wilkenson each a $1,000 bonus for their <u>ordeal</u>.

_____ a. pleasure

_____ b. interview

_____ c. suffering

_____ Score 3 points for each correct C answer.

_____ Score 2 points for each correct O answer.

_____ **Total Score:** Using Words Precisely

Enter the four total scores in the spaces below, and add them together to find your Reading Comprehension Score. Then record your score on the graph on page 73.

Score	Question Type	Lesson 3
_____	Finding the Main Idea	
_____	Recalling Facts	
_____	Making Inferences	
_____	Using Words Precisely	
_____	**Reading Comprehension Score**	

Author's Approach

Put an X in the box next to the correct answer.

1. The author uses the first sentence of the article to
   ☐ a. inform the reader about the Sunshine Silver Mine.
   ☐ b. offer an idea that relates to Chuck Carver's situation on the day of the fire.
   ☐ c. compare the Sunshine Silver Mine's good record to the bad records of other mines.

2. From the statements below, choose those that you believe the author would agree with.
   ☐ a. The rescuers didn't try very hard to find survivors.
   ☐ b. The rescuers did everything they could to save the miners.
   ☐ c. The rescuers were discouraged when all they found were dead bodies.

3. In this article, "In the back of their minds, the miners knew the risks" means the miners
   ☐ a. knew the risks but tried not to think about them.
   ☐ b. had never thought carefully about the risks.
   ☐ c. didn't understand the risks involved.

4. The author tells this story mainly by
   ☐ a. retelling the personal experiences of some of the miners.
   ☐ b. comparing the Sunshine Silver Mine disaster to other mining disasters.
   ☐ c. telling the history of the Sunshine Silver Mine.

_____ Number of correct answers

Record your personal assessment of your work on the Critical Thinking Chart on page 74.

CRITICAL THINKING

Summarizing and Paraphrasing

Follow the directions provided for question 1. Put an X in the box next to the correct answer for question 2.

1. Complete the following one-sentence summary of the article using the lettered phrases from the phrase bank below. Write the letters on the lines.

Phrase Bank:

a. the fire's power and the rescuers' efforts

b. the survival of Flory and Wilkenson

c. a description of the mine and its history

After a short introduction, the article about the Sunshine Silver Mine tragedy begins with _____, goes on to explain _____, and ends with _____.

2. Choose the best one-sentence paraphrase for the following sentence from the article:

"The 12-year veteran miner should have been driving the train that hauls timber and supplies through the underground shafts."

☐ a. The veteran usually drove the train that dropped wood and supplies down the entrance to the mine.

☐ b. The miner was a war veteran who also knew how to drive a train through the underground mine shafts.

☐ c. The experienced miner normally would have driven the train that carried wood and supplies throughout the mine.

_____ Number of correct answers

Record your personal assessment of your work on the Critical Thinking Chart on page 74.

Critical Thinking

Follow the directions provided for questions 1, 3, 4, and 5. Put an X in the box next to the correct answer for question 2.

1. For each statement below, write O if it expresses an opinion and write F if it expresses a fact.

_____ a. Flory and Wilkenson were trapped in the mine for 175 hours.

_____ b. The fire in the Sunshine Silver Mine took more lives than any other mining disaster in the history of Idaho.

_____ c. Mining is the most dangerous job of all.

2. From the information in paragraph 10, you can predict that Flory and Wilkenson would

☐ a. never want to see each other again.

☐ b. remain friends for the rest of their lives.

☐ c. look for a job braiding blasting wire.

3. Choose from the letters below to correctly complete the following statement. Write the letters on the lines.

On the positive side, _____, but on the negative side _____.

a. Chuck Carver was injured a few weeks before the fire

b. Chuck Carver wasn't in the mine when the fire broke out

c. Chuck Carver's replacement, Roberto Diaz, was killed in the fire

4. Choose from the letters below to correctly complete the following statement. Write the letters on the lines.

According to the article, the poisonous fumes from the fire caused _____ to _____, and the effect was _____.

a. dozens of miners

b. they died within a short time

c. black out

5. In which paragraph did you find the information or details to answer question 4?

_____

_____ Number of correct answers

Record your personal assessment of your work on the Critical Thinking Chart on page 74.

Personal Response

How do you think you would feel if you were trapped underground?

_____

_____

_____

_____

Self-Assessment

I can't really understand how

_____

_____

_____

_____

POMPEII
The City That Slept for 1,500 Years

In 1595 a worker digging a tunnel near Naples, Italy, stumbled on a buried town but did nothing about exploring it. More than a hundred years passed before historians identified the buried town. It was Pompeii, an ancient Roman city that had been destroyed and abandoned in A.D. 79.

2   No attempt was made to uncover Pompeii for another half century. Then, in 1748, a Spanish Army engineer became convinced that the city held vast treasure. He obtained permission from the king of Naples to begin excavating the buried city. The excavations turned up treasure of a kind that the engineer never dreamed of.

3   Pompeii had been built on the slope of Mount Vesuvius, an inactive volcano. In A.D. 79, however, Vesuvius became very active indeed. With almost no warning, there was a tremendous explosion inside the volcano.

4   A black cloud shaped like a pine tree formed over Vesuvius. The cloud blotted out the sun. It was as if an eclipse had come to the area. The eruption lasted seven days. Ash, stone, and pieces of hardened lava spurted out of the volcano. On the seventh day, Vesuvius sent out gases that killed all living things within the volcano's reach.

5   The clouds of ash caused lightning storms and rain. Gradually, volcanic ash mixed with mud and rain to form a heavy paste. This paste covered the city to a depth of 12 to 50 feet. It formed a hermetically sealed layer, shutting off oxygen and preventing decay. Beneath the layer of hardened volcanic ash and mud, Pompeii lay in an unbelievably good state of preservation. It was as if the city had been frozen in place. In time, an outer layer of soil covered the layer of paste.

6   Nearly 2,000 years later, excavators uncovered paintings inside homes that were still bright, unfaded by time. Some of the food on tables and shelves was preserved. Loaves of bread were petrified in the ovens. Jugs still held drinkable wine. Figs, raisins, and chestnuts remained in recognizable condition. Olives preserved in oil were still edible.

7   But the most amazing preservations were the remains of many of Pompeii's citizens. The eruption of Mount Vesuvius had given off clouds of lethal gases. The carbon monoxide in the mixture of gases was odorless, but it was deadly. People

Mount Vesuvius is seen in the background through the ruins of the Arch of Nerone in Pompeii, Italy.

When the ash from Vesuvius covered Pompeii and mixed with mud from the rain that followed, many bodies were petrified and preserved for centuries. This photo shows the body of a petrified man.

who hadn't fled from the city died where they stood. Like their possessions, their bodies were covered and preserved by the volcanic ash and mud.

8 Hundreds of years after Vesuvius's eruption, excavators found the petrified body of a Roman soldier. The soldier was fully armed and standing erect. He was found at a guard post in a niche in the city wall. He had remained at his post even though a rain of ash and small stones fell from the sky.

9 The bodies of gladiators who were slain that day are preserved in the volcanic paste. Inside excavated temples, the petrified bodies of priests can be seen. They appear as if frozen while performing their duties.

10 In one home, the diggers found the stonelike remains of a man standing upright. He holds a sword in his hand, and one foot rests on a heap of gold and silver. He seems to have been protecting his wealth from looters. Near him are the bodies of five other men he struck down before he himself was killed by Vesuvius's deadly gases. The volcanic ash preserved the looters and the guardian alike.

11 About 5,000 Pompeians managed to escape the doomed city, and many more tried unsuccessfully to escape. Many tied pillows over their heads for protection against the falling stones and lava, and fled. People who left the city early enough reached the nearby Mediterranean Sea. From its shore they were able to escape in boats. Those who waited too long, however, found that wild tides had swept away the docks and boats, leaving them stranded. Others were struck down before they reached the water.

12 Not all the people in boats were trying to get away from Pompeii. Pliny the Elder was a famous writer as well as commander of the Roman fleet. He was about 200 miles from Pompeii when he heard of the volcanic cloud hanging above Vesuvius. Pliny decided to investigate. He headed for Pompeii with some of his warships. As the ships approached Vesuvius, pieces of burning rock fell on the decks of the vessels. Pliny and his crew landed. They survived the falling rocks for a day, only to be killed by poisonous gas.

13 More than 15,000 of Pompeii's 20,000 people perished. The petrified remains of

about 700 Pompeians can be seen today. Their bodies are on display in the 160,000-acre section of the city that has been excavated.

14 When Pompeii was a living city, it attracted thousands of visitors. Today, the restored city attracts millions of people from all over the world. They marvel at Pompeii's preserved wonders, and for a few hours, they step back 2,000 years to the days when Roman citizens walked the city's streets and lived in its houses. 🍃

If you have been timed while reading this article, enter your reading time below. Then turn to the Words-per-Minute Table on page 71 and look up your reading speed (words per minute). Enter your reading speed on the graph on page 72.

Reading Time: **Lesson 4**

_____ : _____
Minutes   Seconds

A | Finding the Main Idea

One statement below expresses the main idea of the article. One statement is too general, or too broad. The other statement explains only part of the article; it is too narrow. Label the statements using the following key:

M—Main Idea   **B—Too Broad**   **N—Too Narrow**

_____ 1. Volcanic explosions have caused some of the worst disasters in history.

_____ 2. Mount Vesuvius erupted for seven days, spewing ash, rocks, and lava.

_____ 3. A volcanic eruption destroyed the city of Pompeii but also preserved it.

_____ Score 15 points for a correct M answer.

_____ Score 5 points for each correct B or N answer.

_____ **Total Score:** Finding the Main Idea

B | Recalling Facts

How well do you remember the facts in the article? Put an X in the box next to the answer that correctly completes each statement about the article.

1. The first person to discover Pompeii was
   - ☐ a. looking for treasure.
   - ☐ b. digging a foundation.
   - ☐ c. digging a tunnel.

2. When the city was uncovered, some of Pompeii's wines
   - ☐ a. were better-tasting than today's.
   - ☐ b. contained no alcohol.
   - ☐ c. were still drinkable.

3. When Vesuvius started to erupt, Pliny the Elder was
   - ☐ a. in Pompeii.
   - ☐ b. in Rome.
   - ☐ c. about 200 miles away.

4. Mount Vesuvius buried Pompeii in
   - ☐ a. A.D. 79.
   - ☐ b. A.D. 1595.
   - ☐ c. A.D. 1748.

5. Pompeii was covered in a layer of hardened
   - ☐ a. ash and mud.
   - ☐ b. lava.
   - ☐ c. volcanic stone.

Score 5 points for each correct answer.

_____ **Total Score:** Recalling Facts

C Making Inferences

When you combine your own experience and information from a text to draw a conclusion that is not directly stated in that text, you are making an inference. Below are five statements that may or may not be inferences based on information in the article. Label the statements using the following key:

C—Correct Inference   F—Faulty Inference

_____ 1. Gladiators had been fighting just before Vesuvius erupted.

_____ 2. Roman soldiers were loyal to their duty.

_____ 3. Pompeii residents were not afraid of looters breaking into their homes.

_____ 4. Pompeii attracted more people as a living city than it does today.

_____ 5. Volcanoes are accompanied by wild tides.

Score 5 points for each correct answer.

_____ **Total Score:** Making Inferences

D Using Words Precisely

Each numbered sentence below contains an underlined word or phrase from the article. Following the sentence are three definitions. One definition is closest to the meaning of the underlined word. One definition is opposite or nearly opposite. Label those two definitions using the following key. Do not label the remaining definition.

C—Closest   O—Opposite or Nearly Opposite

1. He obtained permission...to begin excavating the buried city.

_____ a. burying

_____ b. digging out

_____ c. measuring

2. It [volcanic ash] formed a hermetically sealed layer, shutting off oxygen and preventing decay.

_____ a. in a sticky way

_____ b. in an airtight way

_____ c. in a way that leaves something exposed to air

3. Loaves of bread were petrified in the ovens.

_____ a. softened

_____ b. baked

_____ c. turned into stone

4. The soldier was fully armed and standing erect.

_____ a. straight up

_____ b. slouched over

_____ c. on a platform

5. He was found at a guard post in a <u>niche</u> in the city wall.

_____ a. remote area

_____ b. raised surface

_____ c. hollowed-out nook

.

_____ Score 3 points for each correct C answer.

_____ Score 2 points for each correct O answer.

_____ **Total Score:** Using Words Precisely

Enter the four total scores in the spaces below, and add them together to find your Reading Comprehension Score. Then record your score on the graph on page 73.

Score	Question Type	Lesson 4
_____	Finding the Main Idea	
_____	Recalling Facts	
_____	Making Inferences	
_____	Using Words Precisely	
_____	**Reading Comprehension Score**	

Author's Approach

Put an X in the box next to the correct answer.

1. The main purpose of the first paragraph is to

☐ a. tell the reader what happened to Pompeii.

☐ b. tell the reader that Pompeii remained hidden for many centuries.

☐ c. tell the reader when historians identified Pompeii.

2. What is the author's purpose in writing "Pompeii: The City That Slept for 1,500 Years"?

☐ a. To encourage the reader to visit Pompeii

☐ b. To inform the reader about what happened to Pompeii

☐ c. To emphasize the similarities between ancient Pompeii and the city today

3. In this article, "It was as if the city had been frozen in place" means

☐ a. Pompeii was covered with a layer of ice.

☐ b. Pompeii seemed very modern.

☐ c. everything in Pompeii looked much as it had in A.D. 79.

4. What does the author imply by saying "The excavations turned up treasure of a kind that the engineer never dreamed of"?

☐ a. The excavations turned up findings that were more valuable than gold.

☐ b. The excavations turned up lots of valuable jewels and coins.

☐ c. The excavations turned up gems and other valuables that the engineer had never seen before.

_____ Number of correct answers

Record your personal assessment of your work on the Critical Thinking Chart on page 74.

Summarizing and Paraphrasing

Follow the directions provided for question 1. Put an X in the box next to the correct answer for question 2.

1. Reread paragraph 12 in the article. Below, write a summary of the paragraph in no more than 25 words.

_____

_____

_____

_____

Reread your summary and decide whether it covers the important ideas in the paragraph. Next, decide how to shorten the summary to 15 words or less without leaving out any essential information. Write this summary below.

_____

_____

_____

2. Choose the best one-sentence paraphrase for the following sentence from the article:

"Those who waited too long, however, found that wild tides had swept away the docks and boats, leaving them stranded."

☐ a. Those who waited too long were swept away by the tides and stranded in the water.

☐ b. Those who waited too long were stuck on land because fierce tides had carried away their boats.

☐ c. Those who waited too long were swept away in their boats by the wild tides.

_____ Number of correct answers

Record your personal assessment of your work on the Critical Thinking Chart on page 74.

Critical Thinking

Follow the directions provided for questions 1, 3, and 4. Put an X in the box next to the correct answer for the other questions.

1. For each statement below, write O if it expresses an opinion and write F if it expresses a fact.

_____ a. More than 15,000 of Pompeii's citizens died after Mount Vesuvius erupted.

_____ b. Pompeii is more interesting today than it was 2,000 years ago.

_____ c. Most of the people who died in Pompeii were killed by a poisonous gas.

2. Judging from Pliny the Elder's actions as told in this article, you can conclude that he was

☐ a. curious and adventurous.

☐ b. cowardly and dishonest.

☐ c. greedy and grasping.

3. Choose from the letters below to correctly complete the following statement. Write the letters on the lines.

In the article, _____ and _____ are different.

a. the condition today of those who escaped Pompeii

b. the condition today of the priests inside excavated temples in Pompeii

c. the condition today of the Roman soldier found at his post in Pompeii

4. Read paragraph 5. Then choose from the letters below to correctly complete the following statement. Write the letters on the lines.

According to paragraph 5, _____ because _____.

a. an outer layer of soil covered the city

b. a heavy paste covering the city prevented decay

c. Pompeii was preserved

5. What did you have to do to answer question 2?

☐ a. find an opinion (what someone thinks about something)

☐ b. find a reason (why something is the way it is)

☐ c. draw a conclusion (a sensible statement based on the text and your experience)

_____ Number of correct answers

Record your personal assessment of your work on the Critical Thinking Chart on page 74.

Personal Response

I wonder why

_____

_____

_____

_____

Self-Assessment

When reading the article, I was having trouble with

_____

_____

_____

_____

CRITICAL THINKING

LONDON FALLS TO ASHES
The Great Fire of London

The Great Fire of London in 1666 burned for 5 days and destroyed much of the city. However, only six people died in the fire.

Just before midnight on September 2, 1666, a fire broke out in one of London's many wooden houses. Some believe it started in Thomas Fraynor's oven. Fraynor, a baker for King Charles II, and his family had been sleeping on the second floor of their Pudding Lane home. They awoke to flames and smoke. Fraynor realized there was only one way out. In a panic, he and his children raced to an upstairs window. They climbed through the opening and along a gutter to the safety of their neighbor's home. A maid working for Fraynor also tried to escape the blaze through the window. But her fear of heights caused her to slip and fall to her death in the street below.

2 About an hour later, unusually strong, dry winds, which had been blowing through London for days, carried the raging fire across the street. Flames ignited piles of hay and straw, and then the Star Inn caught fire. The blaze quickly spread down London streets to the wooden warehouses and sheds along the Thames (TEMZ) River. By morning it had destroyed churches, homes, taverns, and factories. It had also started to sweep across the Old London Bridge.

3 Dazed Londoners fled their homes throughout the night and ran into the streets. They carried their belongings on their heads or backs. Some threw their goods into boats on the river. Their city was literally burning to the ground. The heat of the fire was so intense that the city's pavements actually glowed. Sparks flew everywhere, swirled around by the wind. After the fire's first day, thick yellow smoke blocked out the sun.

4 For a time it looked like Old Saint Paul's Cathedral would be spared. But each day flames crept closer and closer, and soon the landmark was surrounded by fire. The church's roof lit up first. Then streams of molten lead from the roof covering flowed down the sides of the cathedral. Because of the intense heat, stones exploded from the church walls in all directions. Huge chunks of stone and molten lead rolled down city streets making passage impossible. When the cathedral roof finally tumbled down, the shock waves could be felt throughout London.

5 Unfortunately, many Londoners had believed that Old Saint Paul's would survive. In fact, many bet their businesses on it. London had hundreds of booksellers, and most of them had their shops right near the cathedral. Before the fire reached the cathedral, as many books as possible had been stored in an old crypt. But Old Saint Paul's was no match for the great fire. Thousands of books went up in flames. Half-burned pages floated off into the air; some landed dozens of miles from London. Piles of books continued to burn for a full week after the fire was officially declared out.

London in 1616, about 50 years before the fire

6   Although the fire started in the vicinity of London's Thames River, firefighters did not have enough water to fight the blaze. The city got its water from the Thames by a huge water wheel. The wheel lifted water from the river to street level. But the wheel, which was made of wood, was destroyed by the fire. So the people of London organized and formed bucket brigades. They filled wooden pails at the river and passed them along from person to person. But the buckets proved useless. They could not possibly provide enough water to put out the huge fire.

7   Saving the Tower of London became a major concern. Large quantities of gunpowder were stored in the Tower's vaults. If the fire managed to reach the gunpowder, half of London would immediately blow up. The loss of life and property would be enormous. The gunpowder needed to be saved for another reason. It could be used to blow up buildings directly in the fire's path.

8   The Lord Mayor of London supervised the firefighting efforts. He became desperate as the horrible blaze marched on. He instructed firefighters to use poles with hooks to pull down buildings in front of the inferno. By destroying the buildings, he hoped that firebreaks would be created. These areas should have deprived the fire of fuel. Instead, the blaze simply fed on the torn-down structures. The Lord Mayor's plan had failed. The king of England then stepped in. He decided to use gunpowder stored at the Tower of London to create the firebreaks. But his plan failed as well. These firebreaks proved no more useful at stopping the fire than pulling down the buildings with hooks had been.

9   Shortly after the fire began, London's goldsmiths had searched for a safe place to protect their gold. They decided to move it to the Tower of London. Just as the booksellers believed that Old Saint Paul's would be immune to the fire, the goldsmiths also believed that the Tower would be safe. But as the fire neared the building, the goldsmiths realized that the intense heat would melt the gold. They formed a human chain and passed the gold hand to hand to boats waiting on the Thames. The craft carried most of the gold across the river to safety. Meanwhile, fire fighters fought to save the Tower of London from ruin. They won.

10   King Charles and his brother passed among the brave firefighters on the streets and handed them gold coins. This may have encouraged the firefighters, but they knew that their battle against the blaze was hopeless. On the third day of the fire, King Charles and his brother joined the bucket brigades. The royal pair helped to pass along pails of water to throw against the flames. Their help did little good.

11   After five dreadful days, the London fire finally burned itself out. In the end, 463 acres were completely destroyed. That's the area of a large, modern city. A total of 400 streets were wiped out, and 13,000 houses burned to ashes. Nearly 100 churches and several hospitals also had fallen victim to the blaze.

12   Great gains, however, resulted from the fire. A law was passed requiring that all new buildings be made of brick or stone. Hand pumps replaced the wooden buckets that had been so ineffective in battling the blaze. Modern sewers were built under the streets. They replaced filthy, open ditches that used to run down the center of every road and lane. A modern volunteer fire department was also established. But above all, the Black Death, a plague that had been killing thousands of Londoners for hundreds of years, finally ended. The fire killed off the remaining rats and their fleas that spread the dreadful disease. 🍃

If you have been timed while reading this article, enter your reading time below. Then turn to the Words-per-Minute Table on page 71 and look up your reading speed (words per minute). Enter your reading speed on the graph on page 72.

Reading Time: **Lesson 5**

———— : ————
Minutes   Seconds

A | Finding the Main Idea

One statement below expresses the main idea of the article. One statement is too general, or too broad. The other statement explains only part of the article; it is too narrow. Label the statements using the following key:

M—Main Idea **B—Too Broad** **N—Too Narrow**

_____ 1. The Great Fire of London destroyed 13,000 homes and 463 acres.

_____ 2. Fires in cities can cause tremendous damage and hardship.

_____ 3. Although the Great Fire of 1666 destroyed the homes and buildings in London, a renewed city resulted.

_____ Score 15 points for a correct M answer.

_____ Score 5 points for each correct B or N answer.

_____ **Total Score:** Finding the Main Idea

B | Recalling Facts

How well do you remember the facts in the article? Put an X in the box next to the answer that correctly completes each statement about the article.

1. The fire started in
   - ☐ a. the king's own bakery.
   - ☐ b. the king's brother's house.
   - ☐ c. a house belonging to the king's baker.

2. The king's brother
   - ☐ a. was killed by the fire.
   - ☐ b. started the fire.
   - ☐ c. joined the bucket brigade.

3. The fire burned itself out after
   - ☐ a. four days.
   - ☐ b. five days.
   - ☐ c. three days.

4. There wasn't enough water to fight the fire because
   - ☐ a. the water wheel was destroyed by the fire.
   - ☐ b. the buckets caught on fire.
   - ☐ c. nobody was willing to join the bucket brigade.

5. One good thing that resulted from the fire was that the
   - ☐ a. people began to love King Charles II.
   - ☐ b. plague was wiped out.
   - ☐ c. king's baker learned to be more careful with fire.

Score 5 points for each correct answer.

_____ **Total Score:** Recalling Facts

C | Making Inferences

When you combine your own experience and information from a text to draw a conclusion that is not directly stated in that text, you are making an inference. Below are five statements that may or may not be inferences based on information in the article. Label the statements using the following key:

C—Correct Inference   **F—Faulty Inference**

_____ 1. Strong, dry winds helped to spread the blaze.

_____ 2. Londoners were probably very grateful for the Thames River.

_____ 3. Old Saint Paul's Cathedral was able to survive the fire because it was built of stone.

_____ 4. The plague spread more rapidly after the fire.

_____ 5. The fire was started deliberately in order to clean up the city.

Score 5 points for each correct answer.

_____ **Total Score:** Making Inferences

D | Using Words Precisely

Each numbered sentence below contains an underlined word or phrase from the article. Following the sentence are three definitions. One definition is closest to the meaning of the underlined word. One definition is opposite or nearly opposite. Label those two definitions using the following key. Do not label the remaining definition.

C—Closest   **O—Opposite or Nearly Opposite**

1. Their city was <u>literally</u> burning to the ground.

_____ a. fearfully

_____ b. actually

_____ c. not really

2. The heat of the fire was so <u>intense</u> that the city's pavements actually glowed.

_____ a. extremely strong

_____ b. very weak

_____ c. visible

3. Then streams of <u>molten</u> lead from the roof covering flowed down the sides of the cathedral.

_____ a. melted

_____ b. old

_____ c. solid

4. ...the booksellers believed that Old Saint Paul's would be <u>immune to</u> the fire....

_____ a. ruined by

_____ b. responsible for

_____ c. not affected by

5. ...the <u>plague</u> that had been killing off thousands of Londoners for hundreds of years, finally ended.

_____ a. epidemic disease

_____ b. general state of health

_____ c. raging fire

_____ Score 3 points for each correct C answer.

_____ Score 2 points for each correct O answer.

_____ **Total Score:** Using Words Precisely

Enter the four total scores in the spaces below, and add them together to find your Reading Comprehension Score. Then record your score on the graph on page 73.

Score	Question Type	Lesson 5
_____	Finding the Main Idea	
_____	Recalling Facts	
_____	Making Inferences	
_____	Using Words Precisely	
_____	**Reading Comprehension Score**	

Author's Approach

Put an X in the box next to the correct answer.

1. The author uses the first sentence of the article to

☐ a. inform the reader about the housing materials used in London in 1666.

☐ b. tell the reader how the Great Fire of London began.

☐ c. inform the reader about London in 1666.

2. From the statements below, choose those that you believe the author would agree with.

☐ a. King Charles was a proud leader who never mingled with his subjects.

☐ b. Londoners worked together to try to put out the fire.

☐ c. Because so many of the buildings in London were made of wood, sooner or later a terrible fire was bound to occur.

3. From the statement "Great gains, however, resulted from the fire," you can conclude that the author wants the reader to think that

☐ a. in spite of the destruction, the fire had some positive results.

☐ b. the fire was a great tragedy.

☐ c. some people made a great deal of money from the fire.

4. The author tells this story mainly by

☐ a. describing the fire from Thomas Fraynor's point of view.

☐ b. retelling King Charles's personal experiences of the fire.

☐ c. telling how the leaders and the people of London coped with the fire.

_____ Number of correct answers

Record your personal assessment of your work on the Critical Thinking Chart on page 74.

CRITICAL THINKING

Summarizing and Paraphrasing

Follow the directions provided for questions 1 and 2. Put an X in the box next to the correct answer for question 3.

1. Look for the important ideas and events in paragraphs 4 and 5. Summarize those paragraphs in one or two sentences.

_____

_____

_____

2. Complete the following one-sentence summary of the article using the lettered phrases from the phrase bank below. Write the letters on the lines.

> **Phrase Bank:**
> a. how the fire started and spread
> b. the negative and positive results of the fire
> c. the efforts of firefighters and Londoners to put out the blaze

The article about the Great Fire of London begins with _____, goes on to explain _____, and ends with _____.

3. Choose the sentence that correctly restates the following sentence from the article:

"When the cathedral roof finally tumbled down, the shock waves could be felt throughout London."

☐ a. The collapse of the cathedral roof sent out strong vibrations that were felt all over London.

☐ b. People all over London were shocked when the cathedral roof finally fell down.

☐ c. When the cathedral roof fell down, it caused an earthquake that was felt all over London.

> _____ Number of correct answers
>
> Record your personal assessment of your work on the Critical Thinking Chart on page 74.

Critical Thinking

Put an X in the box next to the correct answer for question 1. Follow the directions provided for the other questions.

1. From the article, you can predict that if firefighters hadn't saved the Tower of London,

☐ a. the Lord Mayor would have had the firefighters arrested.

☐ b. the gunpowder in the Tower vault would have blown up.

☐ c. King Charles wouldn't have given gold coins to the firefighters.

CRITICAL THINKING

2. Choose from the letters below to correctly complete the following statement. Write the letters on the lines.

On the positive side, _____, but on the negative side _____.

a. thousands of buildings were destroyed in the fire

b. the fire stopped the plague

c. the king's baker was the first to notice the fire

3. Think about cause-effect relationships in the article. Fill in the blanks in the cause-effect chart, drawing from the letters below.

Cause	Effect
_____	The terrible disease ended in London.
The water wheel was destroyed.	_____
_____	They placed their gold in the Tower.

a. Goldsmiths thought that the Tower of London would be safe from the fire.

b. The fire killed the rats and their fleas that had spread the Black Death.

c. The firefighters didn't have enough water to fight the blaze.

4. Which paragraphs from the article provide evidence that supports your answer to question 3?

_____

_____ Number of correct answers

Record your personal assessment of your work on the Critical Thinking Chart on page 74.

Personal Response

Begin the first 5–8 sentences of your own article about a terrible fire. It may tell of a real experience or one that is imagined.

_____

_____

_____

_____

Self-Assessment

I was confused on question # _____ in section _____ because

_____

_____

_____

_____

CRITICAL THINKING

HINDENBURG
Last of the Great Dirigibles

The *Hindenburg* was a huge, modern, and powerful airship. To the people of Germany, it was a proud symbol of the German nation itself. To Adolf Hitler, it was the showpiece of the new Germany rebuilding itself after its defeat in World War I.

2   Germany had every reason to be proud of the *Hindenburg*. It was the largest airship (also known as a dirigible or a zeppelin) ever built. The great silver dirigible was more than three blocks long. It measured 804 feet from nose to rudder and was marked with huge black Nazi swastikas. Since the *Hindenburg*'s launching in 1936, it had completed 37 ocean crossings.

3   On this crossing in May 1937, the *Hindenburg* was carrying a crew of 61 plus 97 passengers. The passengers had each paid $400, a great deal of money in those days, for the three-day trip. Their $400 let them travel in great comfort and luxury. Dinner included such delicacies as lobster. The list of wines the *Hindenburg* carried was more than a page long. No possible item for the passengers' comfort or safety had been overlooked.

4   Passengers had to give up their own matches and cigarettes when they came

The Hindenburg *explodes at its mooring in Lakehurst, New Jersey, 1937. Inset: The* Hindenburg *sails over New York City in 1937.*

aboard the airship. The *Hindenburg*'s great silver gasbag was filled with hydrogen, a highly flammable gas. The crew was taking no chances. To prevent accidental fire, smoking was permitted only in one completely fireproof room. Metal ladders and railings were encased in rubber to prevent sparks. These precautions resulted in an enviable safety record. No accident had occurred in 14 years of commercial dirigible flights.

5   This flight had started without a hitch. However, by the time it neared its destination, the *Hindenburg* was several hours behind schedule after bucking strong headwinds over the Atlantic. In addition, mooring (tying the airship to a mast) was being delayed by heavy rain. Despite weather conditions, the *Hindenburg* had already passed over New York City and was approaching Lakehurst, about 60 miles from New York City. The *Hindenburg* had tied up at Lakehurst on all previous flights to the United States, and the navy was waiting for it on this trip. Dozens of marines and sailors were on hand to pull in the mooring lines let down from the zeppelin. These long ropes would hold it down until its nose could be secured to the mooring mast.

6   As the airship settled gracefully to the ground, the Lakehurst crew moved forward. Waiting behind them were more

than a thousand spectators who had come, despite the rain, to watch the *Hindenburg* moor. The crowd included newspaper and movie photographers, reporters, and the friends and relatives of

Captain Ernst Lehmann, commander of the Hindenburg, *inspects the construction of the airship prior to its maiden voyage in 1936.*

arriving passengers. They all watched the airship float down like a feather.

7 Boom!

8 There was an explosion and a flash of light from near the *Hindenburg*'s tail. In seconds, the airship had become a great, flaming torch. The huge black swastikas on its tail disappeared in flames. The fiery zeppelin slowly settled to the ground. Members of the ground crew scrambled for their lives. Burning pieces of the *Hindenburg*'s fabric covering fluttered to the ground among the navy men still below the dirigible as it continued its descent.

9 One passenger, Joseph Spahs, an acrobat, leaped to the ground from an open window. He landed unburned and completely unhurt. Other passengers and crew members also leaped from the flaming dirigible and lived. Some, however, were killed by the fall. Others survived the jump only to die later from burns suffered before they leaped.

10 Sailors and marines who had fled from the downward path of the fiery dirigible returned heroically to the airship to pull people from the wreckage. These sailors and marines are credited with saving many lives. One passenger, his clothes completely burned off, was met by the navy men as he walked away from the flames. "I'm completely all right," he said. Then he dropped dead.

11 The *Hindenburg*'s two captains, Ernst Lehmann and Max Pruss, were the last to jump from the flaming wreckage. The *Hindenburg* had had two captains on its fateful trip. Captain Lehmann had commanded the airship in its first voyages. Captain Pruss was in command during this last flight. The hair and clothing of both men were aflame as they left the dirigible's control car. Captain Pruss, though badly burned, lived. Captain Lehmann was not as lucky. Lehmann had been a dirigible pioneer. He had commanded the German zeppelins that had bombed London during World War I. Now, the terribly burned Lehmann kept repeating, "I shall live. I shall live."

12 Despite his statement, Captain Lehmann died within 24 hours. The captain did live long enough, however, to offer his view that the explosion had been caused by sabotage—by a deliberately placed bomb.

13 People still speculate about the cause of the explosion. The official explanation of the Zeppelin Transport Company, which operated the airship, is that static electricity caused by the rainstorm ignited the explosive hydrogen.

14 One member of the United States ground crew had a different explanation.

He saw a ripple—a sort of flutter—in the fabric near the *Hindenburg*'s tail. That flutter may have been caused by escaping hydrogen gas as it passed over the zeppelin's skin. Then, when the engines were thrown into reverse to assist in the landing, sparks were thrown off. Several observers saw sparks that could easily have ignited the flammable gas.

15 What really caused the explosion? Was it escaping hydrogen? Sabotage? Static electricity? We will probably never know the truth. One terrible truth is known; the end of the *Hindenburg* brought an end to the lives of 36 people. It also brought to an end the age of the giant dirigible.

If you have been timed while reading this article, enter your reading time below. Then turn to the Words-per-Minute Table on page 71 and look up your reading speed (words per minute). Enter your reading speed on the graph on page 72.

Reading Time: Lesson 6

_____ : _____

Minutes   Seconds

A Finding the Main Idea

One statement below expresses the main idea of the article. One statement is too general, or too broad. The other statement explains only part of the article; it is too narrow. Label the statements using the following key:

M—Main Idea   B—Too Broad   N—Too Narrow

_____ 1. The explosion of the dirigible *Hindenburg* took 36 lives and ended the commercial use of the dirigible.

_____ 2. The pride of Germany went down in the *Hindenburg*'s flames.

_____ 3. The black swastikas on the *Hindenburg*'s rudder disappeared in the flames.

_____ Score 15 points for a correct M answer.

_____ Score 5 points for each correct B or N answer.

_____ **Total Score:** Finding the Main Idea

B Recalling Facts

How well do you remember the facts in the article? Put an X in the box next to the answer that correctly completes each statement about the article.

1. Smoking was limited aboard the *Hindenburg* because
   ☐ a. Hitler did not approve of smoking.
   ☐ b. hydrogen is very flammable.
   ☐ c. there were no fire extinguishers.

2. The *Hindenburg* arrived late because of
   ☐ a. safety precautions.
   ☐ b. strong headwinds.
   ☐ c. engine trouble.

3. The Zeppelin Transport Company believed the fire resulted from
   ☐ a. sabotage.
   ☐ b. a hydrogen leak near the tail.
   ☐ c. static electricity.

4. When the flaming dirigible began to sink to the ground, United States sailors and marines
   ☐ a. continued to stand beneath it.
   ☐ b. ran to safety but came back to rescue people.
   ☐ c. refused to help the *Hindenburg*'s passengers and crew.

5. The *Hindenburg* had completed
   ☐ a. 37 ocean crossings.
   ☐ b. 40 ocean crossings.
   ☐ c. 10 ocean crossings.

Score 5 points for each correct answer.

_____ **Total Score:** Recalling Facts

C Making Inferences

When you combine your own experience and information from a text to draw a conclusion that is not directly stated in that text, you are making an inference. Below are five statements that may or may not be inferences based on information in the article. Label the statements using the following key:

C—Correct Inference   F—Faulty Inference

_____ 1. The *Hindenburg*'s crew did not follow safety rules.

_____ 2. Traveling by airship was risky but popular.

_____ 3. The *Hindenburg*'s passengers were wealthy.

_____ 4. Captains Lehmann and Pruss were selfish people.

_____ 5. Most of the victims who died were killed in the explosion itself.

Score 5 points for each correct answer.

_____ **Total Score:** Making Inferences

D Using Words Precisely

Each numbered sentence below contains an underlined word or phrase from the article. Following the sentence are three definitions. One definition is closest to the meaning of the underlined word. One definition is opposite or nearly opposite. Label those two definitions using the following key. Do not label the remaining definition.

C—Closest   O—Opposite or Nearly Opposite

1. Dinner included such <u>delicacies</u> as lobster.

_____ a. plain, ordinary food

_____ b. special tasty food

_____ c. fish

2. Metal ladders and railings were <u>encased</u> in rubber to prevent sparks.

_____ a. burned

_____ b. exposed

_____ c. completely covered

3. These precautions resulted in an <u>enviable</u> safety record.

_____ a. predictable

_____ b. desirable

_____ c. unwanted

4. Lehmann had been a dirigible <u>pioneer</u>.

_____ a. a person who does something first

_____ b. a person who does something last

_____ c. a person who questions something

5. People still <u>speculate</u> about the cause of the explosion.

_____ a. report on

_____ b. make guesses about

_____ c. are certain about

_____ Score 3 points for each correct C answer.

_____ Score 2 points for each correct O answer.

_____ **Total Score:** Using Words Precisely

Enter the four total scores in the spaces below, and add them together to find your Reading Comprehension Score. Then record your score on the graph on page 73.

Score	Question Type	Lesson 6
_____	Finding the Main Idea	
_____	Recalling Facts	
_____	Making Inferences	
_____	Using Words Precisely	
_____	**Reading Comprehension Score**	

Author's Approach

Put an X in the box next to the correct answer.

1. What does the author mean by the statement "This flight had started without a hitch"?

☐ a. The dirigible took off with no landing gear.

☐ b. When the flight started, there were no passengers on board.

☐ c. There were no problems when the flight took off.

2. Which of the following statements from the article best describes the *Hindenburg*?

☐ a. "The *Hindenburg* was a huge, modern, and powerful airship."

☐ b. "On this crossing in May 1937, the *Hindenburg* was carrying a crew of 61 plus 97 passengers."

☐ c. "The *Hindenburg*'s great silver gasbag was filled with hydrogen, a highly flammable gas."

3. The author probably wrote this article in order to

☐ a. express an opinion about what caused the *Hindenburg* to explode.

☐ b. tell the reader about dirigibles.

☐ c. inform the reader about the *Hindenburg*'s last flight.

4. How is the author's purpose for writing the article expressed in paragraph 15?

☐ a. The author admits that no one knows exactly what caused the explosion, but it was a terrible and costly disaster.

☐ b. The author reports that 36 people died in the explosion.

☐ c. The author suggests that dirigibles became unpopular after the accident.

_____ Number of correct answers

Record your personal assessment of your work on the Critical Thinking Chart on page 74.

CRITICAL THINKING

Summarizing and Paraphrasing

Put an X in the box next to the correct answer.

1. Below are summaries of the article. Choose the summary that says all the most important things about the article but in the fewest words.

☐ a. On its last flight, the *Hindenburg* flew across the Atlantic to Lakehurst, New Jersey. As it began to descend, however, the dirigible exploded, killing 36 people. Several theories have been proposed to explain the explosion, including escaping hydrogen gas and sabotage. Although no one really knows what caused the explosion, the end of the *Hindenburg* brought an end to the age of the giant dirigibles.

☐ b. The explosion of the *Hindenburg* brought an end to the use of giant dirigibles.

☐ c. After crossing the Atlantic, the *Hindenburg* was due to land in Lakehurst. During the landing, however, the dirigible exploded. Although no one knows what caused the explosion, it brought an end to the age of the giant dirigibles.

2. Read the statement about the article below. Then read the paraphrase of that statement. Choose the reason that best tells why the paraphrase does not say the same thing as the statement.

Statement: To many Germans, the *Hindenburg* was a symbol of their country's growing power and of its ability to rebuild after a humiliating defeat in World War I.

Paraphrase: To the German people, the *Hindenburg* symbolized their country's defeat in World War I.

☐ a. Paraphrase says too much.

☐ b. Paraphrase doesn't say enough.

☐ c. Paraphrase doesn't agree with the statement about the article.

_____ Number of correct answers

Record your personal assessment of your work on the Critical Thinking Chart on page 74.

Critical Thinking

Follow the directions provided for question 1. Put an X in the box next to the correct answer for the other questions.

1. For each statement below, write O if it expresses an opinion and write F if it expresses a fact.

_____ a. Passengers should never have been allowed to travel in dirigibles because these ships are too dangerous.

_____ b. The black swastikas on the *Hindenburg* made it look ugly.

_____ c. Each of the passengers on the *Hindenburg*'s last flight paid $400 for the three-day trip.

2. From what the article told about the *Hindenburg*'s routine landings at Lakehurst, you can conclude that

☐ a. the United States was about to declare war on Germany.

☐ b. relations between the United States and Germany in 1937 were still friendly.

☐ c. the United States supported Adolf Hitler.

3. What was the effect of the strong headwinds over the Atlantic?

☐ a. The crew did not allow passengers to carry their own matches and cigarettes on board the *Hindenburg*.

☐ b. The *Hindenburg* arrived at Lakehurst hours ahead of schedule.

☐ c. The *Hindenburg* was several hours behind schedule.

4. What did you have to do to answer question 3?

☐ a. find an effect (something that happened)

☐ b. find a cause (why something happened)

☐ c. draw a conclusion (a sensible statement based on the text and your experience)

_____ Number of correct answers

Record your personal assessment of your work on the Critical Thinking Chart on page 74.

Personal Response

If you could ask the author of the article one question, what would it be?

_____

_____

_____

_____

Self-Assessment

The part I found most difficult about the article was

_____

_____

_____

_____

I found this difficult because

_____

_____

_____

_____

CRITICAL THINKING

TAKE TO THE HILLS!
The Johnstown Dam Is Going!

The waters from the Johnstown flood flipped this house on its side and deposited a tree in a second floor window.

The rider galloped at top speed down the hill and on into the valley, through the pouring rain. "The dam is going!" A few residents of Johnstown, Pennsylvania, took the rider's advice—and lived. Thousands of people, however, either never got the rider's message or chose to disregard it. Many of those who didn't heed the warning paid with their lives.

2   The citizens of Johnstown in 1889 had good reason for ignoring the advice. Once a year the old South Fork Dam seemed about to burst. The cry, "Take to the hills," had become an annual false alarm.

3   This time, however, the rider's warning should have been taken in earnest. The rider was John G. Parke, a civil engineer who was in charge of the dam.

4   The Great South Fork Dam was a huge earthen dike holding back the waters of an artificial lake. The dam had been constructed without any stone or cement. It had been built by piling up layer upon layer of soil, until the dam was 100 feet high. It was 90 feet wide at its base.

5   The dam had passed through the hands of a series of owners. In recent years the

dam and the lake behind it had been bought by a group of millionaires. The millionaires called themselves the Great South Fork Fishing and Hunting Club. They spent thousands of dollars stocking the lake with fish. They also added screens to prevent the fish from getting out through the dam's drainage holes.

6   Fishing was good, and the lake had never been higher than that spring of 1889. May had been an unusually rainy month. The streets in the lower parts of Johnstown were already flooded with six feet of water. Behind the dam, the lake had been rising at the rate of one foot per hour. The owners of the fishing club sent workers to pile more dirt on top of the dam to keep it from overflowing. The owners also ordered the workers to remove the screens, which had become jammed with fish, sticks, and other debris. The workers tried hard to clear the jam, but John Parke's trained engineer's eye could see that their efforts would be useless. Parke saddled a horse and began his Paul Revere ride through the valley.

7   The rain continued to pour. At noon, the water washed over the top of the dam. Almost immediately a big notch developed in the top of the dike. Then, according to witnesses, the whole dam simply disappeared. One minute there was a dam, and the next minute—nothing.

The lake moved into the valley like a living thing. In little more than half an hour, the dam emptied completely, sending 45 *billion* gallons of water down the valley toward Johnstown. A wave of water reaching 125 feet high raced toward the city, leaping forward at the rate of 22 feet per second.

8   The huge wall of water approached East Conemaugh, a suburb of Johnstown.

As it did, railroad engineer John Hess looked up from the string of freight cars his locomotive was pushing. He saw the water bearing down on him, now moving at 50 miles per hour. Hess moved the locomotive's throttle to wide open. Still pushing a string of freight cars before him, he raced the advancing flood into East Conemaugh. Hess tied down the locomotive's whistle, and its screaming

This photo shows all that was left of the city of Johnstown after the flood.

blast preceded the train into the village. Johnstown was a railroad city. People in the whole Johnstown area knew that a tied-down whistle could only mean a disaster. And the already flooded streets told them what kind of disaster it was. Many people who had ignored earlier warnings now headed for the hills. Unable to reach the center of Johnstown, rail-roader Hess jumped from the locomotive cab in East Conemaugh, ran into his house, and roused his family. The Hesses made their way up the side of a hill just before the flood hit the village.

9   As the great tumbling hill of water roared on toward the center of Johnstown, it ran into the East Conemaugh rail yard. In the yard was a roundhouse containing 37 locomotives. The onrushing flood swept away both roundhouse and engines. The rush of waters was so forceful that it carried the locomotives, weighing 40 tons each, on top of the flood.

10   The rolling mountain of water, now filled with locomotives, freight cars, houses, trees, horses, and humans, rushed on. A great cloud of dust and moisture rolled before the racing floodwaters. The dust cloud was so heavy that many residents of Johnstown never saw the rolling floodwaters behind it. The cloud was quickly named the *death mist*.

11   The mountain of water continued its headlong rush. Just before it reached Johnstown, it destroyed the Gautier Wire Works. The buildings of the wire works and its hundreds of miles of flesh-piercing barbed wire were added to the swirling debris.

12   The giant rolling hill of water rushed into the heart of Johnstown. The flood swept into two distinct parts like the arms of the letter Y. One arm of the flood roared through the residential part of town. Churches, schools, and houses gave way before its power; 800 homes were flushed away.

13   The second arm of the flood, a rumbling mass of houses, trains, people, and animals, swept up to a stone bridge that spanned the valley. The debris caught in the bridge's stone arches and became wedged there. A collection of hundreds of parts of buildings and thousands of residents became hopelessly bound in coils of barbed wire. The water formed a great swirling whirlpool behind them. Hundreds of additional people had approached the whirlpool on makeshift rafts made from pieces of wreckage. They leaped onto the swirling debris, joining the people already trapped there.

14   Then a new horror broke out. Many stoves, their fires still burning, floated into and ignited the mass of debris. Residents on the bridge overhead and on the nearby shore managed to rescue some people by reaching for them with long poles and ropes. Thousands of victims found them-selves trapped between the still rising water and the flames. Some accounts of the flood claim that 200 people committed suicide by deliberately jumping into the flames. They were just a few of the 2,000 to 7,000 people believed to have lost their lives at Johnstown.

15   A week after the flood, a demolition expert placed nine 50-pound cases of dynamite in the debris and cleared the jam. The waters were free to pass under the bridge and continue the 75-mile trip down the valley to Pittsburgh. The people of that city made an astonishing find. The floodwaters had carried a piece of wooden flooring from Johnstown to Pittsburgh. On that bit of wreckage, completely unhurt by the wild ride, was a healthy five-month-old baby. ✑

If you have been timed while reading this article, enter your reading time below. Then turn to the Words-per-Minute Table on page 71 and look up your reading speed (words per minute). Enter your reading speed on the graph on page 72.

Reading Time: Lesson 7

_____ : _____

Minutes   Seconds

A Finding the Main Idea

One statement below expresses the main idea of the article. One statement is too general, or too broad. The other statement explains only part of the article; it is too narrow. Label the statements using the following key:

M—Main Idea   **B—Too Broad**   **N—Too Narrow**

_____ 1. Some people tried to escape the Johnstown flood by making rafts from the wreckage.

_____ 2. All around the world, floods cause loss of life and destruction of property.

_____ 3. The 1889 Johnstown flood which claimed thousands of lives resulted from a combination of natural causes and human error.

_____ Score 15 points for a correct M answer.

_____ Score 5 points for each correct B or N answer.

_____ **Total Score:** Finding the Main Idea

B Recalling Facts

How well do you remember the facts in the article? Put an X in the box next to the answer that correctly completes each statement about the article.

1. Some people didn't believe the dam had burst because
   - ☐ a. flooding was common in Johnstown.
   - ☐ b. there had been too many false alarms.
   - ☐ c. it looked strong enough to last.

2. The number of victims who lost their lives in the flood was
   - ☐ a. 2 to 700.
   - ☐ b. 2,000 to 7,000.
   - ☐ c. 200,000 to 700,000.

3. The dam was owned by the
   - ☐ a. East Conemaugh Railroad.
   - ☐ b. Gautier Wire Works.
   - ☐ c. Great South Fork Fishing and Hunting Club.

4. Wreckage caught in a stone bridge caused the floodwaters to
   - ☐ a. form a whirlpool.
   - ☐ b. switch channels.
   - ☐ c. catch on fire.

5. Many people didn't see the flood coming because
   - ☐ a. it was hidden by a dust cloud.
   - ☐ b. it moved so rapidly.
   - ☐ c. they were sleeping.

Score 5 points for each correct answer.

_____ **Total Score:** Recalling Facts

Making Inferences

When you combine your own experience and information from a text to draw a conclusion that is not directly stated in that text, you are making an inference. Below are five statements that may or may not be inferences based on information in the article. Label the statements using the following key:

C—Correct Inference   F—Faulty Inference

_____ 1. Putting screens over the dam's drainage holes was a mistake.

_____ 2. More lives could have been saved if the locomotive had reached Johnstown earlier.

_____ 3. The millionaires of the Great South Fork Fishing and Hunting Club did nothing to prevent the flood.

_____ 4. Most Johnstown residents didn't believe the dam would burst.

_____ 5. Civil engineer John Parke did his best to warn the residents about the flood.

Score 5 points for each correct answer.

_____ **Total Score:** Making Inferences

D **Using Words Precisely**

Each numbered sentence below contains an underlined word or phrase from the article. Following the sentence are three definitions. One definition is closest to the meaning of the underlined word. One definition is opposite or nearly opposite. Label those two definitions using the following key. Do not label the remaining definition.

C—Closest   O—Opposite or Nearly Opposite

1. Thousands of people, however, either never got the rider's message or chose to disregard it.

_____ a. pay attention to

_____ b. ignore

_____ c. spread

2. This time, however, the rider's warning should have been taken in earnest.

_____ a. seriously

_____ b. undeservedly

_____ c. lightly

3. ...John Parke's trained engineer's eye could see that their efforts would be useless.

_____ a. educated

_____ b. unskilled

_____ c. implanted

4. The mountain of water continued its headlong rush.

_____ a. wonderful

_____ b. reckless

_____ c. thoughtful

5. The debris caught in the bridge's stone arches and became <u>wedged</u> there.

_____ a. stuck

_____ b. loosened

_____ c. destroyed

_____ Score 3 points for each correct C answer.

_____ Score 2 points for each correct O answer.

_____ **Total Score:** Using Words Precisely

Enter the four total scores in the spaces below, and add them together to find your Reading Comprehension Score. Then record your score on the graph on page 73.

Score	Question Type	Lesson 7
_____	Finding the Main Idea	
_____	Recalling Facts	
_____	Making Inferences	
_____	Using Words Precisely	
_____	**Reading Comprehension Score**	

Author's Approach

Put an X in the box next to the correct answer.

1. The main purpose of the first paragraph is to

☐ a. tell the reader how information was communicated in Johnstown.

☐ b. express an opinion about the residents who ignored the rider's advice.

☐ c. prepare the reader for what would happen when the Johnstown dam burst.

2. From the statements below, choose those that you believe the author would agree with.

☐ a. The owners of the dam were more concerned with their fishing club than with the safety of the people of Johnstown.

☐ b. During the flood, people in Johnstown did nothing to try to help each other.

☐ c. An earthen dike is not strong enough to hold back the waters of a lake that is filled to overflowing.

3. In this article, "Parke saddled a horse and began his Paul Revere ride through the valley" means

☐ a. like Paul Revere, who warned the colonists that the British were coming, Parke rode through the valley warning people of the arriving floodwaters.

☐ b. Parke liked to pretend he was Paul Revere when he rode his horse.

☐ c. Parke was joined by Paul Revere as he rode through the valley.

_____ Number of correct answers

Record your personal assessment of your work on the Critical Thinking Chart on page 74.

68

Summarizing and Paraphrasing

Follow the directions provided for question 1. Put an X in the box next to the correct answer for question 2.

1. Reread paragraph 8 in the article. Below, write a summary of the paragraph in no more than 25 words.

_____

_____

_____

_____

Reread your summary and decide whether it covers the important ideas in the paragraph. Next, decide how to shorten the summary to 15 words or less without leaving out any essential information. Write this summary below.

_____

_____

_____

2. Choose the best one-sentence paraphrase for the following sentence from the article:

"The second arm of the flood, a rumbling mass of houses, trains, people, and animals, swept up to a stone bridge that spanned the valley."

☐ a. The flood swept away houses, trains, people, animals, and a bridge that crossed the valley.

☐ b. The second part of the flood rumbled past houses and people but destroyed a bridge that extended across the valley.

☐ c. The second part of the flood, carrying people, houses, and other things with it, moved swiftly up to a bridge that crossed the valley.

_____ Number of correct answers

Record your personal assessment of your work on the Critical Thinking Chart on page 74.

Critical Thinking

Put an X in the box next to the correct answer for questions 1, 4, and 5. Follow the directions provided for the other questions.

1. From the article, you can predict that if John Hess hadn't raced his locomotive into town with the whistle tied down,

☐ a. even more people would have been killed in the flood.

☐ b. the flood would not have swept away the other locomotives in the rail yard.

☐ c. fewer people would have been killed in the flood.

2. Choose from the letters below to correctly complete the following statement. Write the letters on the lines.

In the article, _____ and _____ were alike in their concern for the residents of Johnstown.

a. the people who owned the dam

b. John G. Parke

c. John Hess

3. Choose from the letters below to correctly complete the following statement. Write the letters on the lines.

   According to the article, _____ caused _____, and the effect was _____.

   a.   the mass of debris to ignite

   b.   stoves, with their fires still burning,

   c.   people were trapped between the floodwaters and the flames

4. How is the Johnstown flood an example of a disaster?

   ☐ a.   The flood resulted from the combination of too much rain and poor construction and management of a dam.

   ☐ b.   The flood killed thousands of people and caused widespread damage to property.

   ☐ c.   Demolition experts had to use dynamite to clear the jam at the bridge near Johnstown.

5. If you were an engineer, how could you use the information in the article to build a dam?

   ☐ a.   Build the dam by piling up layer upon layer of soil.

   ☐ b.   Place screens on the dam to keep fish from getting out of the lake behind it.

   ☐ c.   Construct the dam out of stone and cement.

   _____ Number of correct answers

   Record your personal assessment of your work on the Critical Thinking Chart on page 74.

Personal Response

How do you think John Hess felt when he saw the wall of water bearing down on him?

_____

_____

_____

_____

Self-Assessment

One of the things I did best when reading this article was

_____

_____

_____

_____

I believe I did this well because

_____

_____

_____

_____

_____

CRITICAL THINKING

Compare and Contrast

Think about the articles you have read in Unit One. Pick four articles that described the disasters most interesting to you. Write the titles of the articles in the first column of the chart below. Use information you learned from the articles to fill in the empty boxes in the chart.

Title	Who was most affected by this disaster?	What caused the disaster?	What were the long-lasting effects of the disaster?

I would choose to tell a friend about this disaster: _____ because _____

_____

_____

Words-per-Minute Table

Unit One

Directions: If you were timed while reading an article, refer to the Reading Time you recorded in the box at the end of the article. Use this words-per-minute table to determine your reading speed for that article. Then plot your reading speed on the graph on page 72.

Lesson No. of Words	Sample 1098	1 936	2 1075	3 962	4 837	5 1093	6 940	7 1133	Seconds
1:30	732	624	717	641	558	729	627	755	90
1:40	659	562	645	577	502	656	564	680	100
1:50	599	511	586	525	457	596	513	618	110
2:00	549	468	538	481	419	547	470	567	120
2:10	507	432	496	444	386	504	434	523	130
2:20	471	401	461	412	359	468	403	486	140
2:30	439	374	430	385	335	437	376	453	150
2:40	412	351	403	361	314	410	353	425	160
2:50	388	330	379	340	295	386	332	400	170
3:00	366	312	358	321	279	364	313	378	180
3:10	347	296	339	304	264	345	297	358	190
3:20	329	281	323	289	251	328	282	340	200
3:30	314	267	307	275	239	312	269	324	210
3:40	299	255	293	262	228	298	256	309	220
3:50	286	244	280	251	218	285	245	296	230
4:00	275	234	269	241	209	273	235	283	240
4:10	264	225	258	231	201	262	226	272	250
4:20	253	216	248	222	193	252	217	261	260
4:30	244	208	239	214	186	243	209	252	270
4:40	235	201	230	206	179	234	201	243	280
4:50	227	194	222	199	173	226	194	234	290
5:00	220	187	215	192	167	219	188	227	300
5:10	213	181	208	186	162	212	182	219	310
5:20	206	176	202	180	157	205	176	212	320
5:30	200	170	196	175	152	199	171	206	330
5:40	194	165	190	170	148	193	166	200	340
5:50	188	160	184	165	143	187	161	194	350
6:00	183	156	179	160	140	182	157	189	360
6:10	178	152	174	156	136	177	152	184	370
6:20	173	148	170	152	132	173	148	179	380
6:30	169	144	165	148	129	168	145	174	390
6:40	165	140	161	144	126	164	141	170	400
6:50	161	137	157	141	122	160	138	166	410
7:00	157	134	154	137	120	156	134	162	420
7:10	153	131	150	134	117	153	131	158	430
7:20	150	128	147	131	114	149	128	155	440
7:30	146	125	143	128	112	146	125	151	450
7:40	143	122	140	125	109	143	123	148	460
7:50	140	119	137	123	107	140	120	145	470
8:00	137	117	134	120	105	137	118	142	480

Minutes and Seconds

Plotting Your Progress: Reading Speed

Unit One

Directions: If you were timed while reading an article, write your words-per-minute rate for that article in the box under the number of the lesson. Then plot your reading speed on the graph by putting a small X on the line directly above the number of the lesson, across from the number of words per minute you read. As you mark your speed for each lesson, graph your progress by drawing a line to connect the X's.

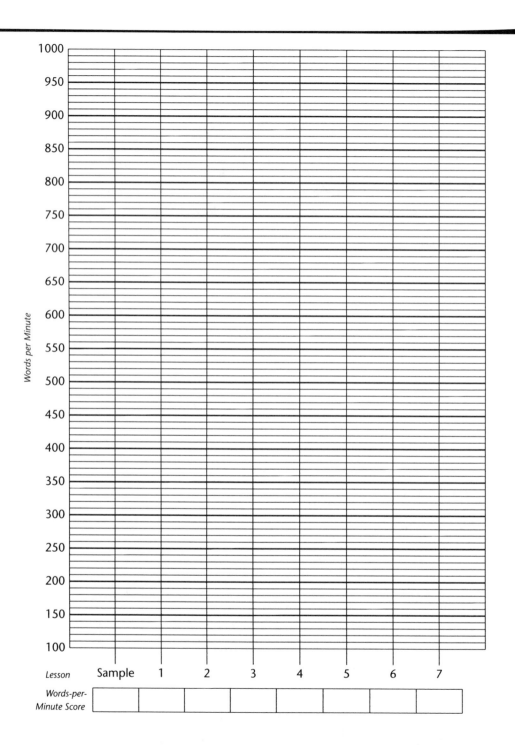

Lesson	Sample	1	2	3	4	5	6	7
Words-per-Minute Score								

Plotting Your Progress: Reading Comprehension

Unit One

Directions: Write your Reading Comprehension score for each lesson in the box under the number of the lesson. Then plot your score on the graph by putting a small X on the line directly above the number of the lesson and across from the score you earned. As you mark your score for each lesson, graph your progress by drawing a line to connect the X's.

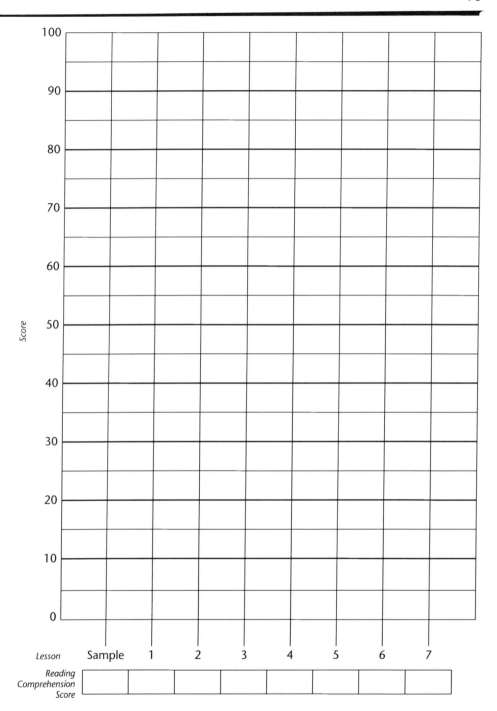

Plotting Your Progress: Critical Thinking

Unit One

Directions: Work with your teacher to evaluate your responses to the Critical Thinking questions for each lesson. Then fill in the appropriate spaces in the chart below. For each lesson and each type of Critical Thinking question, do the following: Mark a minus sign (–) in the box to indicate areas in which you feel you could improve. Mark a plus sign (+) to indicate areas in which you feel you did well. Mark a minus-slash-plus sign (–/+) to indicate areas in which you had mixed success. Then write any comments you have about your performance, including ideas for improvement.

Lesson	Author's Approach	Summarizing and Paraphrasing	Critical Thinking
Sample			
1			
2			
3			
4			
5			
6			
7			

UNIT TWO

DEATH ON THE UNSINKABLE TITANIC

The safest ship afloat." "A seagoing hotel!" "Unsinkable!" These were the words the newspapers used when they wrote about the *Titanic*, the largest ship ever built.

2   The year was 1912. The *Titanic* was on its first trip. It was sailing that April from Southampton, England, to New York City. The captain of the British ship was E. J. Smith, a veteran of many years of trans-atlantic service. Smith wanted to prove that the *Titanic* was not only the world's most luxurious ship but also the fastest. For that reason, Smith held the *Titanic* to a speedy 22 knots for most of the voyage.

3   The *Titanic* carried the very latest in wireless equipment. It received messages from two nearby ships. They warned that they had seen many icebergs. In spite of the warnings, the *Titanic* continued at 22 knots.

4   Lookout Fred Fleet peered ahead from his position high up on the mast. He could see a huge bulk looming in the *Titanic*'s path. Iceberg! Fleet struck three bells—the signal for something dead ahead. First Officer Murdoch, on watch on

The Titanic *disaster captured the attention of the world. Notice the number of people in this photo who are reading newspapers they've just purchased from the newsboy.*

TITANIC DISASTER GREAT LOSS OF LIFE
EVENING NEWS

the bridge, ordered the ship to turn *hard-a-starboard*. At almost the same instant, Murdoch signaled the engine room to stop. The *Titanic* began to turn to one side, as if in slow motion. Too late! With a long, grinding sound, the *Titanic* scraped along the side of the iceberg. The passengers felt almost no shock. The blow was a glancing one; it was almost a near miss. Pieces of ice rained down on one of the *Titanic*'s decks. The passengers, in a holiday mood, felt no sense of danger. After all, everyone knew the *Titanic* was unsinkable. Besides, the crash had been a mere scrape. Card players continued their games. Some passengers sent waiters to pick up chunks of ice from the deck. They used the ice to cool their drinks.

5   Down in the engine room, the crew could see that the *Titanic*'s damage was serious. The berg had ripped a long, jagged gash below the vessel's waterline. The sea was pouring in.

6   The *Titanic* had compartments that divided it into sections from bow to stern. It had been designed so that if any compartment suffered a hole, watertight doors could shut off that section. The undamaged compartments would be more than enough to keep the ship afloat. In fact, if the *Titanic* had struck the iceberg head on, damage would have been much less. At worst, the bow and the first couple of watertight compartments would have been damaged. When the *Titanic* turned to avoid the berg, however, its hull scraped along the berg. A jagged underwater spur of ice had slashed a 300-foot wound in the *Titanic*'s side. Water was pouring into too many of the watertight compartments.

7   In 10 minutes, the water in the forward part of the ship was eight feet deep. Though the ship's pumps had been started up, they were of little help. Below in the firerooms, sweating stokers shoveled coal. They fed the great furnaces of the *Titanic*'s boilers. Those boilers supplied power for the pumps and provided electricity for the lights and the wireless.

8   The engineers and stokers were fighting a losing battle. Water was flooding in much too fast for the pumps. Slowly, the

This traveling bag and its contents were rescued from the Titanic *during exploration of the wreckage in 1987.*

engine room crew retreated before the advancing water. Many of the boilers were flooded out. Enough, however, kept working to furnish electricity for the lights and the wireless.

9   The *Carpathia*, hours away, heard the *Titanic*'s SOS. The *Carpathia* doubled the number of stokers feeding its furnaces. It sent a wireless message to the *Titanic* "Coming hard!"

10   *Titanic*'s captain gave the order to abandon ship. The old rule of the sea—women and children first—was sounded. Not many passengers responded to it. People simply would not believe that the *Titanic*, with its double bottom and watertight compartments, could sink. Many women refused to be parted from their husbands. As a result, the first lifeboats pulled away from the ship only half filled.

11   The sinking *Titanic* was bathed in the glow of distress rockets that it fired every few minutes. Passengers began to understand that the impossible was actually happening. The *Titanic* was going down! The lifeboats were now heavily loaded. And when people realized there would not be nearly enough room in the boats for all of them, they began to panic.

12   The *Titanic*'s bow was deep under water. Its stern rose in the air. The screws—those gigantic propellers that had driven the ship toward a new speed record and toward disaster—were swinging up. Finally they were completely pulled out of the water.

13   People in the lifeboats could see, by the glare of the *Titanic*'s lights, the hundreds of passengers left to their fate aboard the ship. The occupants of the boats watched with a grim fascination. They could see their doomed husbands, relatives, and friends aboard the now rapidly sinking ship. With a great final shudder, the *Titanic* stood on end. Then it plunged beneath the sea.

14   The lifeboats had moved away from the *Titanic*. They wanted to avoid being pulled down by the suction of the sinking ship. The people in the lifeboats assessed their situation. The *Titanic* had been carrying over 2,200 passengers. The lifeboats had a capacity of 1,178. However, in the confusion and in the disbelief that the ship would sink, only 711 people had secured places in the lifeboats.

15   Twenty minutes after the *Titanic* had slid under the sea, the *Carpathia* arrived on the scene in response to the *Titanic*'s SOS. The *Carpathia*'s searchlight probed the night expecting to find the great ship. But the beams of light picked up only small boats—some all but empty—bobbing about on the sea. The unsinkable *Titanic* had carried over 1,500 people with it to a watery grave. The *Carpathia* took the 711 survivors aboard. Then the liner headed for New York at its best speed.

16   The *Titanic* and the passengers and crew members it carried lay undisturbed in their watery grave for almost three quarters of a century. Over those long years, many expeditions searched for the remains of the *Titanic*. In 1986, *Alvin*, a midget sub designed for deep-water exploration, joined the search. *Alvin* succeeded in finding the *Titanic*'s rusty remains. The liner lay in two pieces, more than two and one-half miles down. The ship's bow had plunged 50 feet into the muddy bottom before settling down into the sand. The rear half of the ship, badly broken up, lay some distance away. Scattered about the wreckage for some distance were reminders of the passengers it had carried. Video cameras aboard *Alvin* scanned the sea bottom. They picked up images of bottles of champagne, china cups and saucers, and the head of a little girl's doll.

17   The crew of the midget sub placed a bronze tablet near the *Titanic*'s stern. The marker is in memory of the 1,522 souls who perished with the great ship. May they and the *Titanic* rest in peace.

If you have been timed while reading this article, enter your reading time below. Then turn to the Words-per-Minute Table on page 133 and look up your reading speed (words per minute). Enter your reading speed on the graph on page 134.

Reading Time: Lesson 8

_____ : _____
Minutes   Seconds

A Finding the Main Idea

One statement below expresses the main idea of the article. One statement is too general, or too broad. The other statement explains only part of the article; it is too narrow. Label the statements using the following key:

M—Main Idea   B—Too Broad   N—Too Narrow

_____ 1. Icebergs can do tremendous damage to ships.

_____ 2. Over 1,500 people died when the *Titanic* sank after hitting an iceberg.

_____ 3. An iceberg slashed a 300-foot gash in the *Titanic*'s side.

_____ Score 15 points for a correct M answer.

_____ Score 5 points for each correct B or N answer.

_____ **Total Score:** Finding the Main Idea

B Recalling Facts

How well do you remember the facts in the article? Put an X in the box next to the answer that correctly completes each statement about the article.

1. The *Titanic* was speeding along at 22 knots because
    - ☐ a. the captain wanted to prove it was the world's fastest ship.
    - ☐ b. the crew was unaware that there were icebergs nearby.
    - ☐ c. it was running late.

2. The *Titanic* may not have had as much damage if
    - ☐ a. it had not swerved to avoid the berg.
    - ☐ b. there had been lookouts on duty.
    - ☐ c. it had carried wireless equipment.

3. The iceberg
    - ☐ a. crushed the *Titanic*'s bow and first compartments.
    - ☐ b. crushed the *Titanic*'s stern.
    - ☐ c. slashed open many of the *Titanic*'s watertight compartments.

4. The *Titanic*'s pumps
    - ☐ a. were too small for such a large ship.
    - ☐ b. couldn't keep up with the huge amounts of water pouring in.
    - ☐ c. were out of order.

5. The first lifeboats left the ship only half full because
    - ☐ a. passengers were afraid to board them.
    - ☐ b. people didn't believe that the *Titanic* was sinking.
    - ☐ c. the crew didn't want them overcrowded.

Score 5 points for each correct answer.

_____ **Total Score:** Recalling Facts

C   Making Inferences

When you combine your own experience and information from a text to draw a conclusion that is not directly stated in that text, you are making an inference. Below are five statements that may or may not be inferences based on information in the article. Label the statements using the following key:

C—Correct Inference   **F—Faulty Inference**

_____ 1. The *Titanic* should not have been traveling so fast.

_____ 2. The engineers and stokers couldn't believe the *Titanic* was going to sink.

_____ 3. Passengers showed good judgment when they refused to leave in the first lifeboats.

_____ 4. Captain Smith felt proud of the *Titanic* and confident of its strength.

_____ 5. The rescuing ship, *Carpathia*, expected to arrive before the *Titanic* went under.

Score 5 points for each correct answer.

_____ **Total Score:** Making Inferences

D   Using Words Precisely

Each numbered sentence below contains an underlined word or phrase from the article. Following the sentence are three definitions. One definition is closest to the meaning of the underlined word. One definition is opposite or nearly opposite. Label those two definitions using the following key. Do not label the remaining definition.

C—Closest   **O—Opposite or Nearly Opposite**

1. [Captain] Smith wanted to prove that the *Titanic* was not only the world's most <u>luxurious</u> ship but also the fastest.

_____ a. poor and dull

_____ b. speedy and agile

_____ c. rich and splendid

2. *Titanic's* captain gave the order to <u>abandon</u> ship.

_____ a. leave

_____ b. protect

_____ c. come aboard

3. The occupants of the boats watched with a grim <u>fascination</u>.

_____ a. fear

_____ b. lack of interest

_____ c. strong attraction

4. The people in the lifeboats <u>assessed</u> their situation.

_____ a. ignored

_____ b. took stock of

_____ c. couldn't believe

5. However,…only 711 people had <u>secured</u> places in the boats.

_____ a. obtained

_____ b. lost

_____ c. fought over

_____ Score 3 points for each correct C answer.

_____ Score 2 points for each correct O answer.

_____ **Total Score:** Using Words Precisely

Enter the four total scores in the spaces below, and add them together to find your Reading Comprehension Score. Then record your score on the graph on page 135.

Score	Question Type	Lesson 8
_____	Finding the Main Idea	
_____	Recalling Facts	
_____	Making Inferences	
_____	Using Words Precisely	
_____	**Reading Comprehension Score**	

Author's Approach

Put an X in the box next to the correct answer.

1. Which of the following statements from the article best describes the way engineers had planned the *Titanic* to be sure it would stay afloat?

☐ a. "The *Titanic* carried the very latest in wireless equipment."

☐ b. "After all, everyone knew the *Titanic* was unsinkable."

☐ c. "It had been designed so that if any compartment suffered a hole, watertight doors could shut off that section."

2. From the statement "In spite of the warnings, the *Titanic* continued at 22 knots," you can conclude that the author wants the reader to think that

☐ a. the *Titanic* was the fastest ship in the world.

☐ b. Captain Smith was reckless and didn't think anything could stop the *Titanic*.

☐ c. 22 knots was not very fast.

3. What does the author imply by saying "Some passengers sent waiters to pick up chunks of ice from the deck"?

☐ a. The passengers were panicking.

☐ b. The passengers wanted to study the ice from an iceberg.

☐ c. The passengers were unconcerned by the ship's collision.

4. The author tells this story mainly by

☐ a. comparing the *Titanic* to the *Carpathia*.

☐ b. relating the personal experiences of passengers on board the *Titanic*.

☐ c. reporting on how the passengers and crew on board the *Titanic* reacted to the disaster.

_____ Number of correct answers

Record your personal assessment of your work on the Critical Thinking Chart on page 136.

Summarizing and Paraphrasing

Follow the directions provided for questions 1 and 2. Put an X in the box next to the correct answer for question 3.

1. Look for the important ideas and events in paragraphs 13 and 14. Summarize those paragraphs in one or two sentences.

_____

_____

_____

2. Complete the following one-sentence summary of the article using the lettered phrases from the phrase bank below. Write the letters on the lines.

> **Phrase Bank:**
> a. the ship's sinking
> b. the discovery of the wreckage of the *Titanic* by the *Alvin*
> c. a description of the errors that led to the collision with the iceberg

After a short introduction, the article about the *Titanic* begins with _____, goes on to explain _____, and ends with _____.

3. Read the statement about the article below. Then read the paraphrase of that statement. Choose the reason that best tells why the paraphrase does not say the same thing as the statement.

Statement: When the midget sub *Alvin* found the *Titanic*, its video cameras scanned the sea bottom, recording images of wreckage that called to mind the splendor the great ship and its passengers.

Paraphrase: *Alvin* used its video cameras to photograph the *Titanic*.

☐ a. Paraphrase says too much.

☐ b. Paraphrase doesn't say enough.

☐ c. Paraphrase doesn't agree with the statement about the article.

_____ Number of correct answers

Record your personal assessment of your work on the Critical Thinking Chart on page 136.

Critical Thinking

Put an X in the box next to the correct answer for questions 1, 3, and 4. Follow the directions provided for question 2.

1. Judging from Captain Smith's actions as described in this article, you can predict that

☐ a. no one blamed him for the disaster.

☐ b. some people blamed him for the disaster.

☐ c. he deliberately sabotaged the *Titanic*.

2. Choose from the letters below to correctly complete the following statement. Write the letters on the lines.

   In the article, _____ and _____ are different.

   a.   the fate of those who were picked up by the *Carpathia*

   b.   the fate of those in the lifeboats

   c.   the fate of those who refused to believe the *Titanic* was sinking

3. What was the effect of the passengers' reluctance to get in the lifeboats?

   ☐ a.   Only 711 people secured places in the boats.

   ☐ b.   Many women refused to be parted from their husbands.

   ☐ c.   The *Titanic* sank to a depth of two and one half miles.

4. What did you have to do to answer question 2?

   ☐ a.   make a prediction (what might happen next)

   ☐ b.   find a contrast (how things are different)

   ☐ c.   find an effect (something that happened)

_____ Number of correct answers

Record your personal assessment of your work on the Critical Thinking Chart on page 136.

Personal Response

I can't believe

_____

_____

_____

_____

Self-Assessment

Before reading the article, I already knew

_____

_____

_____

_____

CRITICAL THINKING

HAWAIIAN HURRICANE

Of the seven main Hawaiian islands, Kauai may be the most pristine. Tourists did not begin to discover the island until the 1970s. They were drawn by Kauai's great beauty and uncrowded beaches. The nearby islands of Oahu and Maui had long been tourist hot spots. By comparison, tiny Kauai seemed fresh and unspoiled.

2   Kauai is known as the Garden Island. Its scenery can take your breath away. (The island was the backdrop for two famous movies. These were *South Pacific* and *Jurassic Park*.) Wild orchids bloom all over Kauai. There are crescent-shaped beaches. There are also jungle-draped hillsides and steep cliffs. Many think of the island as "a paradise on Earth."

3   Roughly circular in shape, Kauai is just 30 miles across. Its population is slightly more than 50,000. Kauai has several dormant volcanoes. There are also some beautiful canyons. Mark Twain once called its deep Waimea Canyon "the Grand Canyon of the Pacific." Then there is the cloud-covered Mount Waialeale. With up to 600 inches of rain a year, it is

In 1993, Hurricane Iniki hit the Hawaiian island of Kauai head on and caused extensive damage.

often called the wettest place on Earth. Along the Na Pali coast, waterfalls cascade from the mountains. They fall hundreds of feet down to the ocean.

4   The weather along the coast of Kauai is nearly perfect. People build their houses to take advantage of the gentle, cooling trade winds. They construct large over-hanging roofs to help funnel these breezes into their homes.

5   Also, unlike some other tropical spots, Hawaii rarely gets lashed by hurricanes. One expert explains why: "Strong hurricanes derive their energy from very warm ocean water, above 80 degrees. But the waters surrounding [Hawaii] are generally in the 70s, so storms usually weaken when they get close to the islands."

6   Unfortunately, sometimes there are exceptions to this rule. Once in a great while, a hurricane does strike Hawaii. And the one that hit on September 11, 1993, packed a huge wallop.

7   Hurricane Iniki had been moving along a harmless path. It was well south of Hawaii. But all at once it took a sharp turn, headed north, and made its way straight for Hawaii. Gaining strength as it went, the storm carried torrential rains and wind gusts up to 180 miles per hour.

8   The hurricane dealt only a glancing blow to most of the Hawaiian islands. But

Iniki hit Kauai with its full force. The eye of the storm passed right over the island. "It was a direct hit," said Barbara Hendrie of Hawaii's civil defense office. Iniki turned out to be the worst storm to hit the state in more than a century.

9   The island's striking landscape contributed to the hurricane's destructiveness. Kauai's steep mountains and narrow valleys funneled the winds, making them more intense. The prevalence of overhanging roofs also

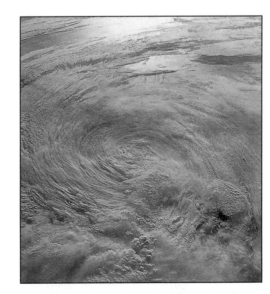

This NASA photo shows a satellite view of Hurricane Iniki as it slams into Kauai.

added to the damage. The winds got underneath these roofs and lifted them off as easily as you open the lid on a can of peanuts. The roofs on thousands of buildings on the island were blown away or damaged. The hurricane even blew the roof off the state government building. Other buildings were completely destroyed by Iniki's winds.

10   Jerry Hill, an amateur radio operator, told of the storm's rage. "All the power lines are down. The telephone communications are out," said Hill. "I can see all the way down to Port Allen from my home here. It's a residential area, and 80 to 90 percent of the homes are damaged severely."

11   The storm flattened fields of sugar cane. It toppled rows of hardwood trees. The brilliant green of the forests became a dull, stumpy brown. Iniki snapped in half the huge smokestack at the Lihue Plantation, the island's largest sugar refinery. It also created monstrous 20-foot ocean waves. These swept cars away. They eroded beaches and washed out coastal roads. Boats anchored at Port Allen Harbor were piled up on top of each other. JoAnn Yukimura, the mayor of Kauai, said, "The destruction was island-wide. Huge chunks of shoreline along the Na Pali coast were washed away, and there is a lot of erosion. It's like the coast aged a century in one day."

12   Iniki also threatened tourists trapped on the island. They had come to Kauai for sun and fun, not a life-and-death adventure. But that's what they got. The hurricane blasted their fancy hotels. Guests were forced to flee inland and wait in long lines at grocery stores to buy food and water. One woman remarked bitterly, "We [have] nothing to eat. There's no electricity, no power, no phone, no nothing." The damage to Kauai's luxury hotels was so extensive that nine months after the hurricane only four of the 11 hotels had reopened.

13   Fortunately, the human cost was fairly light for a storm of this size. Two elderly people died. Hundreds of others were injured and more than 12,000 were left homeless. The hurricane caused more than $1.6 billion in damage.

14   The island's recovery from the storm was painfully slow. For the next couple of years, tourists stayed away. Even though Kauai soon regained its beauty, the island no longer lured them. Hurricane Iniki had turned "a paradise on Earth" into a ruin. Governor John Waihee III said it was "probably the worst disaster we've ever had in the state of Hawaii." No one on the island of Kauai would disagree. 🍃

If you have been timed while reading this article, enter your reading time below. Then turn to the Words-per-Minute Table on page 133 and look up your reading speed (words per minute). Enter your reading speed on the graph on page 134.

Reading Time: Lesson 9

_____ : _____
Minutes   Seconds

A Finding the Main Idea

One statement below expresses the main idea of the article. One statement is too general, or too broad. The other statement explains only part of the article; it is too narrow. Label the statements using the following key:

M—Main Idea   **B—Too Broad**   **N—Too Narrow**

_____ 1. In 1993, Hurricane Iniki slammed into the Hawaiian island of Kauai, causing widespread destruction.

_____ 2. Hurricanes rarely strike the Hawaiian islands.

_____ 3. Hurricane Iniki struck Kauai's luxury hotels, forcing guests to flee inland.

_____ Score 15 points for a correct M answer.

_____ Score 5 points for each correct B or N answer.

_____ **Total Score:** Finding the Main Idea

B Recalling Facts

How well do you remember the facts in the article? Put an X in the box next to the answer that correctly completes each statement about the article.

1. Mark Twain once called Kauai's Waimea Canyon
    ☐ a. "the Grand Canyon of the Pacific."
    ☐ b. "a paradise on Earth."
    ☐ c. "the wettest place on Earth."

2. People on Kauai built large overhanging roofs over their houses to
    ☐ a. help capture rainwater.
    ☐ b. protect their homes from hurricanes.
    ☐ c. help funnel cool breezes into their homes.

3. The eye of Hurricane Iniki passed right over
    ☐ a. Kauai.
    ☐ b. Maui.
    ☐ c. Oahu.

4. In 1993, JoAnn Yukimura was
    ☐ a. an amateur radio operator.
    ☐ b. the mayor of Kauai.
    ☐ c. an employee in Hawaii's civil defense office.

5. In human terms, Hurricane Iniki killed
    ☐ a. hundreds of people and injured 12,000 others.
    ☐ b. two people and injured hundreds of others.
    ☐ c. no one but caused many injuries.

Score 5 points for each correct answer.

_____ **Total Score:** Recalling Facts

C | Making Inferences

When you combine your own experience and information from a text to draw a conclusion that is not directly stated in that text, you are making an inference. Below are five statements that may or may not be inferences based on information in the article. Label the statements using the following key:

C—Correct Inference   F—Faulty Inference

_____ 1. Houses on Kauai were constructed to withstand powerful hurricanes.

_____ 2. For several years after Iniki, tourists feared that another hurricane could strike Kauai without warning.

_____ 3. It will take a long time for Kauai to regain its reputation as a "paradise on Earth."

_____ 4. Many houses in Kauai were severely damaged by Iniki.

_____ 5. Since the hurricane, tourists have avoided all of the Hawaiian islands.

Score 5 points for each correct answer.

_____ **Total Score:** Making Inferences

D | Using Words Precisely

Each numbered sentence below contains an underlined word or phrase from the article. Following the sentence are three definitions. One definition is closest to the meaning of the underlined word. One definition is opposite or nearly opposite. Label those two definitions using the following key. Do not label the remaining definition.

C—Closest   O—Opposite or Nearly Opposite

1. Of the seven main Hawaiian islands, Kauai may be the most <u>pristine</u>.

_____ a. polluted

_____ b. far away

_____ c. unspoiled

2. Kauai has several <u>dormant</u> volcanoes.

_____ a. inactive

_____ b. energetic

_____ c. steep

3. Gaining strength as it went, the storm carried <u>torrential</u> rains and wind gusts up to 180 m.p.h.

_____ a. freezing

_____ b. violently rushing

_____ c. light

4. They <u>eroded</u> beaches and washed out coastal roads.

_____ a. built up

_____ b. wore away

_____ c. visited

5. Even though Kauai soon regained its beauty, the island no longer <u>lured</u> them.

_____ a. repelled

_____ b. frightened

_____ c. attracted

_____ Score 3 points for each correct C answer.

_____ Score 2 points for each correct O answer.

_____ **Total Score:** Using Words Precisely

Enter the four total scores in the spaces below, and add them together to find your Reading Comprehension Score. Then record your score on the graph on page 135.

Score	Question Type	Lesson 9
_____	Finding the Main Idea	
_____	Recalling Facts	
_____	Making Inferences	
_____	Using Words Precisely	
_____	**Reading Comprehension Score**	

Author's Approach

Put an X in the box next to the correct answer.

1. The main purpose of the first paragraph is to

☐ a. describe the qualities of Kauai.

☐ b. describe the beauty of the Hawaiian Islands.

☐ c. encourage the reader to visit Kauai.

2. From the statement "Its scenery can take your breath away," you can conclude that the author wants the reader to think that

☐ a. people have difficulty breathing on Kauai.

☐ b. the island has a high elevation.

☐ c. Kauai is a very beautiful place.

3. What does the author imply by saying "They had come to Kauai for sun and fun, not a life-and-death adventure"?

☐ a. The hurricane took tourists by surprise.

☐ b. The tourists who came to Kauai liked to take risks.

☐ c. Many tourists had fun on Kauai in spite of the hurricane.

4. The author probably wrote this article in order to

☐ a. describe the beautiful island of Kauai.

☐ b. tell the reader about a terrible hurricane that struck Kauai.

☐ c. convey a mood of sadness about the destruction caused by Iniki.

_____ Number of correct answers

Record your personal assessment of your work on the Critical Thinking Chart on page 136.

CRITICAL THINKING

Summarizing and Paraphrasing

Put an X in the box next to the correct answer.

1. Below are summaries of the article. Choose the summary that says all the most important things about the article but in the fewest words.

☐ a. Hurricane Iniki slammed into the island of Kauai on September 11, 1993. Kauai, known as the Garden Island, suffered terrible damage. Many homes and buildings were also destroyed. Fortunately, though, the cost in human life was fairly light.

☐ b. In 1993, Hurricane Iniki changed its course and struck the island of Kauai.

☐ c. Hurricane Iniki struck Kauai in 1993. The hurricane severely damaged the beautiful island and destroyed a great deal of property. Iniki also damaged Kauai's reputation among tourists.

2. Choose the sentence that correctly restates the following sentence from the article:

"The winds got underneath these roofs and lifted them off as easily as you might take the lid off a can."

☐ a. The winds scattered cans and other debris on the roofs of houses.

☐ b. The strong winds easily blew the roofs off the houses.

☐ c. When the winds got underneath the roofs, people could easily lift them off the houses.

_____ Number of correct answers

Record your personal assessment of your work on the Critical Thinking Chart on page 136.

Critical Thinking

Put an X in the box next to the correct answer.

1. From what the article told about Kauai, you can predict that

☐ a. the island will probably not suffer devastating hurricanes every year.

☐ b. from now on, severe hurricanes will continue to hit the island regularly.

☐ c. the island's residents will move to other Hawaiian islands.

2. What was the effect of Kauai's steep mountains and narrow valleys on Hurricane Iniki?

☐ a. The eye of the storm passed right over the island.

☐ b. The hurricane turned sharply to the north and headed straight for Hawaii.

☐ c. The mountains and valleys funneled the winds, making them more intense.

3. If you were an architect in Kauai, how could you use the information in the article to build and design houses?

☐ a. Decrease the amount of hurricane damage by designing houses without overhanging roofs.

☐ b. Decrease the amount of hurricane damage by building houses along coastal areas.

☐ c. Decrease the amount of hurricane damage by building houses in valleys.

CRITICAL THINKING

4. What did you have to do to answer question 2?

☐ a. find an effect (something that happened)

☐ b. find a purpose (why something is done)

☐ c. draw a conclusion (a sensible statement based on the text and your experience)

_____ Number of correct answers

Record your personal assessment of your work on the Critical Thinking Chart on page 136.

Personal Response

What new question do you have about this topic?

_____

_____

_____

Self-Assessment

One of the things I did best when reading this article was

_____

_____

_____

_____

I believe I did this well because

_____

_____

_____

_____

CRITICAL THINKING

SAN JUAN'S TOWERING INFERNO

Medical personnel remove a body from the Dupont Plaza Hotel after a New Year's Eve fire destroyed the hotel. A total of 97 people died in the inferno.

It was early in the afternoon of December 31, 1986. Most of the guests in the Dupont Plaza Hotel in San Juan, Puerto Rico, had come to party and celebrate New Year's Eve. Some rested in their rooms, anticipating a late night. Others gathered in the casino to test their luck. Still others took a leisurely swim in the hotel's pool. No one knew what horrors awaited them.

2   But there were warning signs of trouble brewing. Over the last 10 days, four small but suspicious fires had broken out. During two of these fires, guests had to be evacuated. Also, there were rumors that, as Puerto Rican governor Rafael Colón later put it, "something was going to happen" at the hotel.

3   And then there were the frightening phone calls to some of the guests. Alfredo Vertz, for instance, got a phone call in his room from an anonymous woman. "I'm going to burn you and everyone else in the hotel," the voice threatened. A few other guests got similar calls.

4   Freda Fenner, staying at a guesthouse next door, was warned not to go into the

Dupont Plaza. A hotel worker told her, "Don't even think about going [in the hotel.] There is going to be a bombing."

5   At least one couple checked out of the Dupont Plaza because of these rumors. But hotel officials reassured other guests that there was nothing to fear; they had everything under control. To be on the safe side, the hotel even hired 30 extra security guards.

6   The threats were coming from a few workers at the Dupont Plaza. Their union was locked in a very bitter dispute with management. The workers were planning to go on strike at midnight on New Year's Eve. The union used a radio advertisement to scare tourists away from the hotel. The message was a dire one: The Dupont Plaza "will not be a good place" to celebrate New Year's Eve.

7   That turned out to be an understatement. At 3:20 P.M., another fire broke out at the hotel. This one had been set deliberately by three hotel employees. And this time they made sure the fire wouldn't be easily put out. In the South Ballroom, they ignited cardboard boxes and a pile of combustible furniture. Quickly the fire and its acrid black smoke spread to the North Ballroom. In most hotels this would have triggered fire alarms and the sprinkler system. But

neither of these safety features had been installed at the Dupont Plaza Hotel. Under the Puerto Rican building codes at the time, neither was required. As a result, most of the guests remained totally unaware of the growing inferno.

8   The smoke from the South Ballroom began to filter into the adjoining casino through air ducts. At first, many guests paid no attention to the smoke. They were focused on their gambling. "People were still sitting there playing the slots with the smoke swirling around them," said Kevin Gibson. Meanwhile, the immense heat of the blaze in the South Ballroom caused its thick glass windows to explode. As people became aware of the billowing smoke, they ran screaming for the exits. But many of the doors were closed, and people were forced back by the smoke.

9   José Aponte was playing cards in the far end of the casino. He tried to remain calm. He quickly gathered his chips and headed for one of the exits. The thick smoke, however, blocked his path. Then, with the temperature inside the casino soaring, he glanced up at the ceiling. Aponte could tell that the fire was moving along the acoustic tiles. They were turning black and advancing in his direction. "I got scared," Aponte later said. "It's a fear beyond panic when you are 100 percent

sure that if you don't do something, you are going to be dead in a minute."

10   Aponte grabbed a wooden stool and tried to smash the heavy plate-glass window above the pool area. He banged it several times but couldn't break it. Then

Smoke billows from the Dupont Plaza Hotel.

another man picked up a metal stool and smashed a small hole in the window. Aponte crawled through to a ledge on the other side. It was a 20-foot drop, and Aponte was hesitant to jump. Then he looked back into the building. He saw a huge ball of fire raging through the casino, incinerating everything in its path. "I knew everybody inside the casino was killed," he said, "because the screaming stopped." Aponte jumped. He broke his ankle in the fall, but he had saved his life.

11   Meanwhile, the deadly blaze continued to spread throughout the 22-floor Dupont Plaza. Some people managed to get to the roof of the hotel. There they found themselves stranded, with the smoke and flames coming ever closer to them.

12   The only way to rescue these people was by helicopter. But that wouldn't be easy. The winds and brutal updrafts caused by the heat made controlling a helicopter very difficult. Also, the hotel roof wasn't one big flat surface. There was a large superstructure with the name "Dupont Plaza" in the middle of it. So pilots couldn't just land on the roof; there wasn't enough room. They would have to hover their aircraft at an angle to avoid having the blades hit the superstructure. If they were lucky, they might manage to get one of the helicopter's landing skids onto the edge of the roof. One slight mistake, however, and the blade would hit the superstructure, sending the helicopter crashing into the people on the roof or to the ground below.

13   Despite the dangers, pilots Julio Colón, Angel Rojas, José Maldonado, and Pat Walter made many rescue trips. Other pilots also helped out. With each trip they managed to get a few people off the roof. It took more than four hours to rescue everyone. In all, more than 160 people made it to the roof and onto a helicopter.

14   The Dupont Plaza inferno was one of the worst hotel fires in memory. In all, 97 people died, including 86 in the casino. Some of those in the casino were found still sitting in their seats, burned beyond recognition. Most of the others died when they became trapped in the hotel's elevators. More than 140 other guests were injured in the fire.

15   The police quickly proved that arson was the cause of the fire. The three employees who set the blaze were caught in less than three weeks. They were members of the local union. These individuals pleaded guilty and were sentenced to prison terms ranging from 75 to 99 years.

If you have been timed while reading this article, enter your reading time below. Then turn to the Words-per-Minute Table on page 133 and look up your reading speed (words per minute). Enter your reading speed on the graph on page 134.

Reading Time: Lesson 10

_____ : _____
Minutes   Seconds

A | Finding the Main Idea

One statement below expresses the main idea of the article. One statement is too general, or too broad. The other statement explains only part of the article; it is too narrow. Label the statements using the following key:

M—Main Idea   **B—Too Broad**   **N—Too Narrow**

_____ 1. Some workers at the Dupont Plaza wanted to damage the hotel to demonstrate their anger with management.

_____ 2. José Aponte escaped the blaze by breaking a window and jumping 20 feet to the ground.

_____ 3. A fire set by angry employees at the Dupont Plaza Hotel in San Juan trapped and killed many of the hotel's guests.

_____ Score 15 points for a correct M answer.

_____ Score 5 points for each correct B or N answer.

_____ **Total Score:** Finding the Main Idea

B | Recalling Facts

How well do you remember the facts in the article? Put an X in the box next to the answer that correctly completes each statement about the article.

1. Many of the guests at the Dupont Plaza Hotel had come to celebrate
   ☐ a. Christmas.
   ☐ b. Easter.
   ☐ c. New Year's Eve.

2. Some guests received threatening phone calls from
   ☐ a. workers at the Dupont Plaza.
   ☐ b. the management of the Dupont Plaza.
   ☐ c. Puerto Rican governor Rafael Colón.

3. The fire started
   ☐ a. on the hotel's roof.
   ☐ b. in the South Ballroom.
   ☐ c. in the North Ballroom.

4. When smoke first began to filter into the casino, many people
   ☐ a. panicked and ran screaming for the exits.
   ☐ b. tried to break windows in order to get out.
   ☐ c. paid no attention and continued gambling.

5. Helicopter pilots could not land their aircraft on the hotel's roof because
   ☐ a. there were too many people waiting to be rescued.
   ☐ b. a large superstructure bearing the hotel's name rose in the middle of the roof.
   ☐ c. the roof was on fire.

Score 5 points for each correct answer.

_____ **Total Score:** Recalling Facts

C | Making Inferences

When you combine your own experience and information from a text to draw a conclusion that is not directly stated in that text, you are making an inference. Below are five statements that may or may not be inferences based on information in the article. Label the statements using the following key:

C—Correct Inference   F—Faulty Inference

_____ 1. The helicopter pilots risked their lives to save the people on the hotel's roof.

_____ 2. In spite of the threats, before the fire most of the hotel guests didn't believe that they were in any danger.

_____ 3. The hotel employees who set the fire didn't mean to do any harm.

_____ 4. The Dupont Plaza was equipped to handle fires.

_____ 5. Guests who escaped from the casino had a better chance of surviving the fire.

Score 5 points for each correct answer.

_____ **Total Score:** Making Inferences

D | Using Words Precisely

Each numbered sentence below contains an underlined word or phrase from the article. Following the sentence are three definitions. One definition is closest to the meaning of the underlined word. One definition is opposite or nearly opposite. Label those two definitions using the following key. Do not label the remaining definition.

C—Closest   O—Opposite or Nearly Opposite

1. During two of these fires, guests had had to be <u>evacuated</u>.

   _____ a. retained

   _____ b. reported

   _____ c. removed

2. Alfredo Vertz, for instance, got a phone call in his room from an <u>anonymous</u> woman.

   _____ a. unknown

   _____ b. familiar

   _____ c. rude

3. The message was a <u>dire</u> one: The Dupont Plaza "will not be a good place" to celebrate New Year's Eve.

   _____ a. loud

   _____ b. comforting

   _____ c. alarming

4. Quickly the fire and its <u>acrid</u> black smoke spread to the North Ballroom.

   _____ a. sweet

   _____ b. bitter

   _____ c. heavy

5. He saw a huge ball of fire raging through the casino, <u>incinerating</u> everything in its path.

_____ a. burning up

_____ b. frightening

_____ c. extinguishing

_____ Score 3 points for each correct C answer.

_____ Score 2 points for each correct O answer.

_____ **Total Score:** Using Words Precisely

Enter the four total scores in the spaces below, and add them together to find your Reading Comprehension Score. Then record your score on the graph on page 135.

Score	Question Type	Lesson 10
_____	Finding the Main Idea	
_____	Recalling Facts	
_____	Making Inferences	
_____	Using Words Precisely	
_____	**Reading Comprehension Score**	

Author's Approach

Put an X in the box next to the correct answer.

1. What does the author mean by the statement "That [message] turned out to be an understatement"?

☐ a. The reality was worse than the message suggested it would be.

☐ b. The message greatly exaggerated the situation.

☐ c. The message was hard to understand.

2. What is the author's purpose in writing "San Juan's Towering Inferno"?

☐ a. To inform the reader about a terrible fire in a Puerto Rican hotel

☐ b. To inform the reader about safety hazards in Puerto Rican hotels

☐ c. To inform the reader about labor disputes in Puerto Rico

3. How is the author's purpose for writing the article expressed in paragraph 7?

☐ a. The author tells the reader that Puerto Rican building codes didn't require fire alarms or sprinkler systems.

☐ b. The author tells the reader how the fire in the hotel got started.

☐ c. The author tells the reader about the conflict between the hotel employees and management.

4. Choose the statement below that best describes the author's position in paragraph 13.

☐ a. The helicopter pilots were foolish to attempt such a mission.

☐ b. The helicopter pilots made a heroic effort to save people.

☐ c. The helicopter pilots were very slow.

_____ Number of correct answers

Record your personal assessment of your work on the Critical Thinking Chart on page 136.

CRITICAL THINKING

Summarizing and Paraphrasing

Follow the directions provided for questions 1 and 2. Put an X in the box next to the correct answer for question 3.

1. Look for the important ideas and events in paragraphs 9 and 10. Summarize those paragraphs in one or two sentences.

_____

_____

_____

2. Complete the following one-sentence summary of the article using the lettered phrases from the phrase bank below. Write the letters on the lines.

> **Phrase Bank:**
> a. warning signs that trouble was brewing at the hotel
> b. the helicopter pilots' rescue efforts
> c. how the fire started and spread through the hotel

After a short introduction, the article about the Dupont Plaza fire begins with _____, goes on to explain _____, and ends with _____.

3. Choose the best one-sentence paraphrase for the following sentence from the article:

"One slight mistake, however, and the blade would hit the superstructure, sending the helicopter crashing into the people on the roof or to the ground below."

☐ a. If the pilot made a mistake, the helicopter would send the superstructure crashing onto the roof or to the ground below.

☐ b. If the pilot made a mistake, the superstructure would crush the people on the roof or fall to the ground below.

☐ c. If the pilot made a mistake, the helicopter blade would hit the superstructure and the helicopter would fall on the people on the roof or onto the ground below.

> _____ Number of correct answers
>
> Record your personal assessment of your work on the Critical Thinking Chart on page 136.

Critical Thinking

Put an X in the box next to the correct answer for questions 1 and 4. Follow the directions provided for the other questions.

1. From the events in the article, you can predict that the following will happen next:

☐ a. The Puerto Rican building codes will require that fire alarms and sprinkler systems be installed in all public buildings.

☐ b. Labor unions in Puerto Rico will become feared and powerful.

☐ c. The Dupont Plaza Hotel will close its casino.

2. Choose from the letters below to correctly complete the following statement. Write the letters on the lines.

On the positive side, _____, but on the negative side _____.

   a. José Aponte could tell that the fire was moving along the ceiling tiles

   b. José Aponte survived the fire

   c. José Aponte broke his ankle

3. Think about cause-effect relationships in the article. Fill in the blanks in the cause-effect chart, drawing from the letters below.

Cause	Effect
_____	One couple checked out of the hotel.
There were no fire alarms in the hotel.	_____
Immense heat built up in the South Ballroom.	_____

   a. Its thick glass windows exploded.

   b. Rumors spread throughout the hotel that something bad was going to happen.

   c. The guests didn't realize that the hotel was on fire.

4. How is the Dupont Plaza inferno an example of a disaster?

   ☐ a. The fire was the result of a labor union dispute.

   ☐ b. Many innocent people died or were injured in the tragic fire.

   ☐ c. Guests had to be evacuated during the fire.

_____ Number of correct answers

Record your personal assessment of your work on the Critical Thinking Chart on page 136.

Personal Response

What would you have done when smoke began to fill the hotel's casino?

_____

_____

_____

_____

Self-Assessment

The part I found most difficult about the article was

_____

_____

_____

I found this difficult because

_____

_____

_____

_____

CRITICAL THINKING

KRAKATOA
The Doomsday Crack Heard 'Round the World

In August 1883, the people of Texas heard a tremendous boom that they thought was cannon fire. What the Texans actually heard was the sound of a series of volcanic eruptions on Krakatoa, an island halfway around the world in the South Pacific. The sound from Krakatoa (now part of Indonesia) was the loudest noise in human history.

2 Krakatoa was a small island—only six miles square—between Java and Sumatra. It almost disappeared from the face of the earth, and the noise of its passing was heard halfway around the world. On Borneo, 350 miles from Krakatoa, the islanders believed the sound was caused by an evil spirit seeking revenge. Terrified, they managed to escape from the spirit, but only by jumping off a cliff and killing themselves.

3 Noise was not the volcano's only way of announcing its eruption. A cloud of steam and ash rose to a height of more than 36,000 feet—more than 7 miles. A ship more than 15 miles from Krakatoa was covered with volcanic ash 15 feet deep. Ash fell on ships as far as 1,600

What used to be the island of Krakatoa is now an underwater volcano, shown erupting in these photos.

miles from Krakatoa and eventually covered an area of 300,000 square miles.

4　Some of the lava that also spewed from the volcano mixed with air and hardened into a stone called *pumice*. The air in pumice makes it so light that it floats. Pumice from Krakatoa was blown into the sea where ocean currents spread it over a large area of the Pacific. For 18 months after the eruption, ships plowed through seas covered with great chunks of floating pumice. Then the pumice stones absorbed so much water that they lost their buoyancy and sank.

5　The volcano's light volcanic ash and dust rose into the atmosphere where winds carried it all over the earth. Weather all over the globe was affected for months after the eruption. For an entire year, the umbrella of dust permitted only 87 percent of the usual amount of sunlight to reach the earth. For two years, the reflection of the sun on the ash in the upper atmosphere resulted in spectacular sunsets. Sunsets were blue in South America and green in Panama. The skies over the United States glowed so red that people thought the color was the result of gigantic fires. People turned in fire alarms in Poughkeepsie, New York, and in New Haven, Connecticut.

6　The great shock wave generated by the eruption swept completely around the world and kept right on going. It circled the globe once—twice—seven times in all.

7　Krakatoa's eruption was accompanied by a great earthquake. The quake jolted the seabed under the waters surrounding the island. The seas around Krakatoa rose to a temperature 60 degrees Fahrenheit above normal. A *tsunami* (tsoo-NAH-mee), a giant sea wave, rolled toward the island.

The tsunami reached a height of 135 feet and attained a speed of 600 miles per hour.

8　It was this great hill of moving water that caused most of the 36,000 casualties associated with Krakatoa. The wave spread out in all directions and wiped out more than 300 villages in Southeast Asia. The tsunami picked up a gunboat and dropped it at a point 30 feet above sea level and more than a mile inland. All the gunboat's crew members were killed.

This engraving shows the island and volcano of Krakatoa before the eruption.

9   Giant tidal waves raced from Krakatoa to all parts of the globe. Their effects were felt as far away as the English Channel, some 13,000 miles.

10   Krakatoa itself was torn to pieces. Five cubic miles of rock—as much as in some of the world's tallest mountains—were blown into dust. Three-fourths of the island disappeared into dust and air. Those parts of the island that didn't explode into the air sank into the sea. Parts of the island that had been a thousand feet above sea level now lay a thousand feet under the ocean.

11   After the eruption, the small piece of Krakatoa that was left was covered with volcanic dust. There was no grass, no shrubs, no trees. A single red spider—the only living thing that survived the eruption—spun its web, a web for which there were no more insects.

12   In 1925 a small peak popped up out of the sea next to Krakatoa. More and more of the peak emerged from the sea until a new island was formed. The South Pacific islanders named the newcomer *Anak Krakatoa*, Child of Krakatoa. In 1928, three years after its birth, Anak Krakatoa had a minor eruption. The island continues to emerge from the sea and to grow larger and larger.

13   What will be the fate of Anak Krakatoa? Will it grow into a full-sized island? Will it have a gigantic volcanic eruption? Only time will tell. 🍃

If you have been timed while reading this article, enter your reading time below. Then turn to the Words-per-Minute Table on page 133 and look up your reading speed (words per minute). Enter your reading speed on the graph on page 134.

Reading Time: Lesson 11

_____ : _____
Minutes   Seconds

A | Finding the Main Idea

One statement below expresses the main idea of the article. One statement is too general, or too broad. The other statement explains only part of the article; it is too narrow. Label the statements using the following key:

M—Main Idea   **B—Too Broad**   **N—Too Narrow**

_____ 1. The terrible effects of volcanic eruptions on Krakatoa in 1883 were felt around the world.

_____ 2. Krakatoa is a dramatic example of the power of volcanoes.

_____ 3. When Krakatoa erupted, volcanic ash fell on ships as far away as 1,600 miles from the island.

_____ Score 15 points for a correct M answer.

_____ Score 5 points for each correct B or N answer.

_____ **Total Score:** Finding the Main Idea

B | Recalling Facts

How well do you remember the facts in the article? Put an X in the box next to the answer that correctly completes each statement about the article.

1. The tremendous eruptions on Krakatoa could be heard as far away as
   - ☐ a. Borneo.
   - ☐ b. Texas.
   - ☐ c. Java and Sumatra.

2. Volcanic ash from Krakatoa covered a ship to a depth of
   - ☐ a. 15 inches.
   - ☐ b. 15 feet.
   - ☐ c. 15 yards.

3. Pumice stones from Krakatoa
   - ☐ a. covered large portions of the Atlantic Ocean.
   - ☐ b. sank ships in the Pacific Ocean.
   - ☐ c. drifted until they became waterlogged and sank.

4. Most of the casualties were caused by
   - ☐ a. a giant wave.
   - ☐ b. volcanic ash and dust.
   - ☐ c. pumice stones.

5. The skies over the United States turned
   - ☐ a. blue.
   - ☐ b. red.
   - ☐ c. green.

Score 5 points for each correct answer.

_____ **Total Score:** Recalling Facts

C | Making Inferences

When you combine your own experience and information from a text to draw a conclusion that is not directly stated in that text, you are making an inference. Below are five statements that may or may not be inferences based on information in the article. Label the statements using the following key:

C—Correct Inference   F—Faulty Inference

_____ 1. Each time a shock wave from Krakatoa circled the earth it gained in strength.

_____ 2. People in Poughkeepsie, New York, and New Haven, Connecticut, turned in fire alarms when they heard the explosion.

_____ 3. Parts of Krakatoa ended up about a thousand feet below sea level.

_____ 4. Before Krakatoa's volcano erupted, no one had ever heard of pumice.

_____ 5. The story suggests that it is just a matter of time before Krakatoa will erupt again.

Score 5 points for each correct answer.

_____ **Total Score:** Making Inferences

D | Using Words Precisely

Each numbered sentence below contains an underlined word or phrase from the article. Following the sentence are three definitions. One definition is closest to the meaning of the underlined word. One definition is opposite or nearly opposite. Label those two definitions using the following key. Do not label the remaining definition.

C—Closest   O—Opposite or Nearly Opposite

1. Some of the lava that also <u>spewed from</u> the volcano mixed with air and hardened into…pumice.

_____ a. fell into

_____ b. burst out of

_____ c. burned holes into

2. Then the pumice stones absorbed so much water that they lost their <u>buoyancy</u> and sank.

_____ a. tendency to float

_____ b. tendency to sink

_____ c. tendency to turn colors

3. The great shock wave <u>generated</u> by the eruption swept completely around the world….

_____ a. destroyed

_____ b. predicted

_____ c. produced

4. The tsunami…<u>attained</u> a speed of 600 miles per hour.

_____ a. failed to achieve

_____ b. reached

_____ c. erupted at

5. The island continues to <u>emerge from</u> the sea and to grow larger and larger.

_____ a. pollute

_____ b. rise out of

_____ c. descend into

_____ Score 3 points for each correct C answer.

_____ Score 2 points for each correct O answer.

_____ **Total Score:** Using Words Precisely

Enter the four total scores in the spaces below, and add them together to find your Reading Comprehension Score. Then record your score on the graph on page 135.

Score	Question Type	Lesson 11
_____	Finding the Main Idea	
_____	Recalling Facts	
_____	Making Inferences	
_____	Using Words Precisely	
_____	**Reading Comprehension Score**	

Author's Approach

Put an X in the box next to the correct answer.

1. The author uses the first sentence of the article to
   - ☐ a. inform the reader about Texas in 1883.
   - ☐ b. describe a noise heard in Texas in 1883.
   - ☐ c. emphasize the similarities between the sound of cannon fire and a volcanic eruption.

2. What is the author's purpose in writing "Krakatoa: The Doomsday Crack Heard 'Round the World"?
   - ☐ a. To tell the reader about the volcanic eruptions that destroyed Krakatoa
   - ☐ b. To inform the reader about tsunamis
   - ☐ c. To describe the sound made by the volcanic eruptions that destroyed Krakatoa

3. What does the author imply by saying "For an entire year, the umbrella of dust permitted only 87 percent of the usual amount of sunlight to reach the earth"?
   - ☐ a. For a year, the earth was brighter and warmer than usual.
   - ☐ b. For a year, the earth was darker and cooler than usual.
   - ☐ c. For a year, the sun didn't shine at all on the earth.

11

4. Choose the statement below that best describes the author's position in paragraph 13.

- [ ] a. The author claims that only time will tell what the fate of Anak Krakatoa will be.

- [ ] b. The author claims that Anak Krakatoa will have a gigantic volcanic eruption someday.

- [ ] c. The author claims that, in time, Anak Krakatoa will grow into a full-sized island.

_____ Number of correct answers

Record your personal assessment of your work on the Critical Thinking Chart on page 136.

Summarizing and Paraphrasing

Put an X in the box next to the correct answer.

1. Below are summaries of the article. Choose the summary that says all the most important things about the article but in the fewest words.

- [ ] a. In 1883, a violent series of volcanic eruptions on the island of Krakatoa produced a noise heard halfway around the world.

- [ ] b. In 1883, volcanic eruptions and a tsunami destroyed the island of Krakatoa, resulting in about 36,000 casualties. The eruptions sent shock waves around the world and affected the weather all over the globe.

- [ ] c. In 1883, a violent series of volcanic eruptions destroyed the island of Krakatoa. The eruptions were accompanied by a tsunami, which caused most of the 36,000 casualties associated with Krakatoa. Volcanic ash from the eruptions was carried all over the earth, resulting in spectacular sunsets in many parts of the world.

2. Choose the sentence that correctly restates the following sentence from the article:

"A single red spider—the only living thing that survived the eruption—spun its web, a web for which there were no more insects."

- [ ] a. The only thing to survive the eruption was a spider web and a few insects.

- [ ] b. The only living thing to survive the eruption was a spider caught in its own web.

- [ ] c. The only living thing to survive the eruption was a spider, whose web would catch no insects.

_____ Number of correct answers

Record your personal assessment of your work on the Critical Thinking Chart on page 136.

Critical Thinking

Follow the directions provided for questions 1 and 3. Put an X in the box next to the correct answer for the other questions.

1. For each statement below, write O if it expresses an opinion and write F if it expresses a fact.

_____ a. The sound made by the eruptions on Krakatoa was the loudest noise in human history.

_____ b. For two years after the eruptions, sunsets were green in Panama.

_____ c. A volcanic eruption will destroy Anak Krakatoa someday.

CRITICAL THINKING

2. From the information in paragraph 11, you can predict that

☐ a. the spider would soon die because it had nothing to eat.

☐ b. birds would soon eat the spider.

☐ c. insects would soon be attracted to the spider's web.

3. Choose from the letters below to correctly complete the following statement. Write the letters on the lines.

According to the article, _____ caused _____, and the effect was _____.

a. volcanic ash and dust to rise into the atmosphere

b. Krakatoa's eruptions

c. weather around the world was affected for months

4. How is the series of volcanic eruptions on Krakatoa an example of a disaster?

☐ a. The eruptions caused the loudest noise ever known.

☐ b. The eruptions caused unusual sunsets around the world.

☐ c. The eruptions caused the deaths of at least 36,000 people and destroyed an island.

5. What did you have to do to answer question 2?

☐ a. find an opinion (what someone thinks about something)

☐ b. make a prediction (what might happen next)

☐ c. find a reason (why something is the way it is)

_____ Number of correct answers

Record your personal assessment of your work on the Critical Thinking Chart on page 136.

Personal Response

What was most surprising or interesting to you about this article?

_____

_____

_____

_____

Self-Assessment

Which concepts or ideas from the article were difficult to understand?

_____

_____

_____

_____

Which were easy to understand?

_____

_____

_____

_____

CRITICAL THINKING

HALIFAX
City Blown to Pieces

The United States and Canada shipped vast quantities of war material to the Allies during World War I. Millions of tons of munitions passed through the Canadian port of Halifax, Nova Scotia. Because the citizens of the city feared an attack by German *zeppelins* (dirigibles or airships), artillery batteries had been set along the shore. To prevent underwater attacks, antisubmarine nets had been strung at the entrance to the harbor. That harbor was reached by way of a long channel only a mile wide. The channel was appropriately named "the narrows."

2 On the morning of December 6, 1917, a French ship, the *Mont Blanc*, was threading its way through the channel. It was bound for Europe with a load of munitions. The *Mont Blanc* was a floating bomb. Its cargo consisted of 7,000 tons of TNT and other explosives, plus 9,000 gallons of benzene, a highly flammable liquid.

3 Heading toward the *Mont Blanc* in "the narrows" was a freighter, the *Imo*, returning empty from Belgium. The *Imo* blew its whistle to signal that it would

pass the *Mont Blanc* to starboard. For some reason never explained, the *Imo* continued on straight toward the *Mont Blanc*. The captain of the *Mont Blanc* realized that he couldn't get his ship out of the *Imo*'s path. He did, however, manage to maneuver the vessel so that the approaching ship would not strike its cargo of TNT. The *Imo*'s bow sliced the *Mont Blanc* all the way down to the waterline. It also sliced open the *Mont*

Blanc's cargo of benzene. The highly flammable liquid spilled into the ship's hold, where it caught fire. The blazing fuel flowed toward the 7,000 tons of explosives.

4 The *Mont Blanc*'s crew knew that their lives depended on putting out the flames. Although the French sailors fought desperately, the rapidly spreading flames drove them back, foot by foot. The captain realized that the struggle was

Canadian soldiers search the ruins of the Halifax harbor and surrounding city for victims of the explosion.

A man stands next to all that remains of his home after the explosion in the Halifax harbor.

hopeless and gave the order to abandon ship. The crew needed no urging. They knew that it was a life-or-death matter to get clear of the ship before it blew up. They rowed for their lives. When their boat reached the shore, they jumped out and kept right on fleeing.

5   The *Mont Blanc* and its explosive cargo drifted toward the piers of Halifax. A British warship, the *High Flyer*, had been waiting to convoy the *Mont Blanc* to Europe and protect it from attack by German subs. Now the crew aboard the *High Flyer* realized that it was the city of Halifax that needed protecting—and from the *Mont Blanc*. A boatload of British sailors set out for the blazing vessel, intending to sink it before it could explode. They reached the burning ship and had just climbed to its deck when the *Mont Blanc* blew up with a boom heard six miles away. It simply disappeared. Many citizens of Halifax were sure that the long-expected zeppelin bombing was under way. Other residents believed that the German navy had crossed the Atlantic and was shelling them.

6   At least two-thirds of the sailors on the ships in Halifax harbor died instantly. The *Mont Blanc*'s blast set off other explosions among the stacks of munitions on the piers. About 3,000 acres—including homes, factories, and schools—were destroyed by the explosions and the fires that followed them. Only 10 pupils out of 500 survived the blast. It is thought that a total of 1,600 people lost their lives and 8,000 were badly injured. The exact death toll will never be known, however, since some entire families were wiped out.

7   A telegrapher named Vincent Coleman played one of the most heroic roles that day in a city of heroes. Coleman saw a ship on fire and realized that it was the munitions ship scheduled to dock that morning. He telegraphed: "A munitions ship is on fire and headed for Pier Eight. Goodbye." It was truly goodbye for Coleman; he died in the explosion. His message, however, started help on the way within 15 minutes of the blast. People from all over Canada and from the north-eastern United States sent food, blankets, cots, medical supplies, lumber, and window glass. The survivors soon had most of the things they needed.

8   One survivor of the disaster was the steamship *Imo* which had rammed the *Mont Blanc*. When the *Mont Blanc* exploded, the Imo was blown clear out of the water onto the shore. The ship was rebuilt and refloated under a new name. Four years after the Halifax explosion, the *Imo* struck a reef in the South Atlantic and sank.

9   The city of Halifax itself emerged successfully from the disaster. There was little of the rioting and looting so common in calamities in other locations. In fact, there were many examples of charity and selfless care for one another. For example, druggists gave away free medical supplies and restaurants provided free meals. Halifax was soon named "The City of Comrades." Working together as comrades, the survivors of Halifax soon rebuilt their town. Today's Halifax is a strong and modern city. 🍃

If you have been timed while reading this article, enter your reading time below. Then turn to the Words-per-Minute Table on page 133 and look up your reading speed (words per minute). Enter your reading speed on the graph on page 134.

Reading Time: **Lesson 12**

_____ : _____

Minutes   Seconds

A Finding the Main Idea

One statement below expresses the main idea of the article. One statement is too general, or too broad. The other statement explains only part of the article; it is too narrow. Label the statements using the following key:

M—Main Idea   **B—Too Broad**   **N—Too Narrow**

_____ 1. Transporting explosives can be very dangerous.

_____ 2. A munitions ship blew up during World War I and severely damaged Halifax.

_____ 3. The explosions and fires destroyed homes, factories, and schools in Halifax.

_____ Score 15 points for a correct M answer.

_____ Score 5 points for each correct B or N answer.

_____ **Total Score:** Finding the Main Idea

B Recalling Facts

How well do you remember the facts in the article? Put an X in the box next to the answer that correctly completes each statement about the article.

1. The people of Halifax feared
☐ a. a zeppelin raid.
☐ b. an explosion in the harbor.
☐ c. a land invasion by the German army.

2. The *Mont Blanc's* crew
☐ a. carelessly caused the explosion.
☐ b. got away safely.
☐ c. were able to keep the fire under control.

3. The crew of the British warship *High Flyer* intended to
☐ a. sink the *Mont Blanc* before the fire reached the TNT.
☐ b. tow the *Mont Blanc* out of the harbor.
☐ c. fight the fire aboard the *Mont Blanc*.

4. Telegrapher Vincent Coleman
☐ a. managed to escape the blast.
☐ b. started help on the way.
☐ c. warned *Mont Blanc's* crew that the ship was going to explode.

5. The *Imo* survived the explosion because the ship
☐ a. sailed away before the explosion.
☐ b. had no cargo and floated high in the water.
☐ c. was blown onto the shore.

Score 5 points for each correct answer.

_____ **Total Score:** Recalling Facts

C │ Making Inferences

When you combine your own experience and information from a text to draw a conclusion that is not directly stated in that text, you are making an inference. Below are five statements that may or may not be inferences based on information in the article. Label the statements using the following key:

C—Correct Inference   F—Faulty Inference

_____ 1. Telegrapher Vincent Coleman suspected that he was doomed.

_____ 2. *Mont Blanc*'s captain was a cool-headed man.

_____ 3. The people of Halifax were selfish and did not care about the future of their town.

_____ 4. Schools were located not far from the harbor.

_____ 5. The *Mont Blanc* was a lucky ship.

Score 5 points for each correct answer.

_____ **Total Score:** Making Inferences

D │ Using Words Precisely

Each numbered sentence below contains an underlined word or phrase from the article. Following the sentence are three definitions. One definition is closest to the meaning of the underlined word. One definition is opposite or nearly opposite. Label those two definitions using the following key. Do not label the remaining definition.

C—Closest   O—Opposite or Nearly Opposite

1. ...a French ship, the *Mont Blanc*, was <u>threading</u> its way through the channel.

_____ a. carefully moving

_____ b. standing still

_____ c. exploding

2. Its cargo consisted of...9,000 gallons of benzene, a highly <u>flammable</u> liquid.

_____ a. prized

_____ b. fireproof

_____ c. easily set on fire

3. He [the captain] did, however, manage to <u>maneuver</u> the vessel so that the approaching ship would not strike its cargo of TNT.

_____ a. empty

_____ b. skillfully guide

_____ c. clumsily misdirect

4. The *High Flyer* had been waiting to <u>convoy</u> the *Mont Blanc* to Europe and protect it from attack by German subs.

_____ a. escort or guard

_____ b. abandon or desert

_____ c. arrest

5. Working together as <u>comrades</u>, the survivors of Halifax soon rebuilt their town.

_____ a. friends

_____ b. prisoners

_____ c. enemies

_____ Score 3 points for each correct C answer.

_____ Score 2 points for each correct O answer.

_____ **Total Score:** Using Words Precisely

Enter the four total scores in the spaces below, and add them together to find your Reading Comprehension Score. Then record your score on the graph on page 135.

Score	Question Type	Lesson 12
_____	Finding the Main Idea	
_____	Recalling Facts	
_____	Making Inferences	
_____	Using Words Precisely	
_____	**Reading Comprehension Score**	

Author's Approach

Put an X in the box next to the correct answer.

1. What does this statement mean? "A telegrapher named Vincent Coleman played one of the most heroic roles that day in a city of heroes"

☐ a. Vincent Coleman, among others, acted heroically that day.

☐ b. Many war heroes, including Vincent Coleman, lived in Halifax.

☐ c. Vincent Coleman only pretended to be a hero.

2. The main purpose of the first paragraph is to

☐ a. inform the reader about World War I.

☐ b. describe the citizens' fear of attack by Germany.

☐ c. describe Halifax harbor and activities there during World War I.

3. Which of the following statements best describes Halifax?

☐ a. "Now the crew aboard the *High Flyer* realized that it was the city of Halifax that needed protecting—and from the *Mont Blanc*."

☐ b. "Halifax was soon named 'The City of Comrades.'"

☐ c. "Many citizens of Halifax were sure that the long-expected zeppelin bombing was under way."

4. From the statement "When their boat reached the shore, they jumped out and kept right on fleeing," you can conclude that the author wants the reader to think that

☐ a. the members of the *Mont Blanc* crew were cowards.

☐ b. the members of the *Mont Blanc* crew feared that they would be blamed for the disaster that was near at hand.

☐ c. the piers of Halifax were in danger from the *Mont Blanc*.

_____ Number of correct answers

Record your personal assessment of your work on the Critical Thinking Chart on page 136.

CRITICAL THINKING

Summarizing and Paraphrasing

Follow the directions provided for questions 1 and 2. Put an X in the box next to the correct answer for question 3.

1. Look for the important ideas and events in paragraphs 2 and 3. Summarize those paragraphs in one or two sentences.

    _____

    _____

    _____

2. Reread paragraph 8 in the article. Below, write a summary of the paragraph in no more than 25 words.

    _____

    _____

    _____

    _____

Reread your summary and decide whether it covers the important ideas in the paragraph. Next, decide how to shorten the summary to 15 words or less without leaving out any essential information. Write this summary below.

    _____

    _____

    _____

3. Choose the best one-sentence paraphrase for the following sentence from the article:

    "Although the French sailors fought desperately, the rapidly spreading flames drove them back, foot by foot."

    ☐ a. The French sailors wanted to fight each other, but the fire drove them away.

    ☐ b. The French sailors battled the fire, but the flames kept burning their feet.

    ☐ c. The French sailors battled the fire, but the flames kept driving them back.

    _____ Number of correct answers

    Record your personal assessment of your work on the Critical Thinking Chart on page 136.

Critical Thinking

Put an X in the box next to the correct answer for question 1. Follow the directions provided for the other questions.

1. From what the article told about the *Imo*, you can predict that

    ☐ a. many people would blame the ship's captain for the disaster in Halifax.

    ☐ b. most of the *Imo*'s crew would survive the *Mont Blanc*'s explosion.

    ☐ c. the ship would be taken over by the German navy.

CRITICAL THINKING

2. Choose from the letters below to correctly complete the following statement. Write the letters on the lines.

   On the positive side, _____, but on the negative side _____.

   a. the *Imo* struck a reef in the South Atlantic and sank

   b. thousands of Halifax residents were killed or injured in the harbor explosions

   c. Halifax was rebuilt and today is a strong and modern city

3. Think about cause-effect relationships in the article. Fill in the blanks in the cause-effect chart, drawing from the letters below.

Cause	Effect
_____	He gave the order to abandon ship.
The *High Flyer* wanted to protect Halifax.	_____
Help arrived soon after the blast.	_____

   a. The captain of the *Mont Blanc* realized that it was useless to fight the fire in his ship's hold.

   b. Coleman telegraphed that the munitions ship was on fire.

   c. A boatload of sailors went to put out the fire on the *Mont Blanc.*

4. Which paragraphs from the article provide evidence that supports your answer to question 3?

   _____

   _____ Number of correct answers

   Record your personal assessment of your work on the Critical Thinking Chart on page 136.

Personal Response

Describe a time when another community worked together in a time of disaster.

_____

_____

_____

_____

Self-Assessment

A word or phrase in the article that I do not understand is

_____

_____

_____

_____

CRITICAL THINKING

THE NIGHT A TOWN DISAPPEARED

A hole 700 feet wide and 200 feet deep resulted when tons of clay collapsed into an underground stream in St.-Jean-Vianney, Quebec, Canada.

The small warning signs went completely unnoticed. Cracks appeared on streets and driveways. Telephone poles sometimes began to sway when there was no wind at all. One man painted the exposed part of his home's foundation, but by the following spring, the ground next to the house had sunk more than half a foot, leaving the unpainted section of the foundation exposed. Other people heard loud thumps or the sound of running water beneath their homes. They looked out their windows and checked their basements. Seeing nothing out of the ordinary, they shrugged off these weird occurrences.

2   Then, on the night of May 4, 1971, the dogs in this small Canadian village went crazy. Most of the dogs in Saint-Jean-Vianney, Quebec, were well-behaved—but not this night. They all began sniffing the ground, running wildly in circles, and barking incessantly. There appeared to be no reason for their odd behavior. Yet none of the usual methods that owners used to calm down the dogs worked. One woman lost her patience. "[My dog] yapped to go

out and yapped to come in. Finally I slapped him."

3   It was too bad the people of this quiet village 135 miles north of the city of Quebec couldn't understand dog talk. It might have saved their lives. What the 1,308 residents didn't know was that the dogs could sense the ground moving under the village. The animals' instinctive fear of the shifting earth was causing their strange behavior.

4   There was good reason to be afraid. The village of Saint-Jean-Vianney had been built on the site of a massive landslide that had occurred 500 years earlier. But it wasn't the kind of slide in which the land pours down the side of a mountain. The land in this part of Quebec is fairly flat. Beneath the topsoil, however, there was a 100-foot deep layer of unstable clay, which was heavily pockmarked with patches of sand. When sand like this becomes saturated with moisture, it can cause the clay to dissolve and liquefy. Then the clay will flow like a river.

5   Although no one knew it, that was what was happening under Saint-Jean-Vianney in May 1971. It had rained often in April. The water didn't run off, but rather seeped into the ground. Also, there had been a rapid early thaw, melting the snow pack. This water, too, soaked into the ground. The infusion of all this water was dissolving the clay.

6   Most of the residents of Saint-Jean-Vianney were home on the night of May 4. Children were sleeping. Most of the adults were watching the Stanley Cup hockey playoffs on television. It was raining hard.

7   At 10:45 P.M., the clay began to move. Suddenly the lights in the homes went out, and the TV screens went blank. "A car must have hit a power pole," said one man. But then he walked outside to take a look around. He saw a bus half swallowed by a hole in the road. He saw that there was only a black void where his neighbor's

A car is perched at the edge of the massive crater in St.-Jean-Vianney.

house had once stood. Running back into the house, he shouted, "The Laval house is gone.... We must leave. NOW!"

8   The Laval house was swept away as the ground beneath it dissolved. What had seemed solid land moments before was now a fast-flowing river of clay in a deep crater. Everything went—the house, the car, and the Lavals. One by one, the mother and the three children disappeared beneath the surface. The river of clay stripped off the father's clothes and smashed him into the roots of a standing tree. Somehow, the tree held firm and he was able to pull himself out of the crater.

9   Robert Paquette also stepped outside his house to see why the lights had been extinguished. He left behind his wife and five children. Up the street, he saw people shouting and waving so Paquette rushed up to join them. A neighbor screamed at Paquette and pointed back in the direction of his house. Paquette turned and saw his home swirl and disappear from sight, taking with it all the members of his family. "I don't understand," Paquette cried in anguish. "I don't understand."

10   Jules Girard was driving a bus that ferried workers home from a nearby aluminum plant. He was steering the bus across a crack in the pavement when the front end of the vehicle suddenly dropped into a hole. Girard could see the road ahead sinking before his eyes. "Everyone out the back door!" he ordered. "Quick!" Girard himself was the last one out, and he barely made it. As he turned to look at the bus, all he could see was its red roof lights. Moments later, Girard watched in horror as a car approaching the crater from the other side plunged into the opening. Apparently, that driver never saw the hole.

11   Around midnight the disastrous landslide ended. The hellish nightmare was over. The deadly river of clay hardened and then stopped. But by then the oozing clay had sucked away 38 houses. Thirty-one men, women, and children had gone under with them. A rescue helicopter pilot described what he saw from above. "The whole area just dropped straight down, leaving sheer sides," said Maurice Roy. "Along with the houses, the entire road had disappeared.

From the helicopter all you can see is this huge crater."

12   Three weeks later, the Canadian government declared the entire village unfit for habitation. Most of the residents were moved, at no cost, to a new community in nearby Arvida. The name of Saint-Jean-Vianney disappeared from atlases and road maps. It would live on only in the memories of those who survived that dreadful night of May 4, 1971. 🍃

If you have been timed while reading this article, enter your reading time below. Then turn to the Words-per-Minute Table on page 133 and look up your reading speed (words per minute). Enter your reading speed on the graph on page 134.

Reading Time: Lesson 13

_____ : _____
Minutes   Seconds

A | Finding the Main Idea

One statement below expresses the main idea of the article. One statement is too general, or too broad. The other statement explains only part of the article; it is too narrow. Label the statements using the following key:

M—Main Idea   B—Too Broad   N—Too Narrow

_____ 1. In 1971, the village of Saint-Jean-Vianney suffered a strange disaster.

_____ 2. In May 1971, the earth caved in and swallowed up the village of Saint-Jean-Vianney.

_____ 3. Robert Paquette saw his home—and all of his family—disappear under the earth.

_____ Score 15 points for a correct M answer.

_____ Score 5 points for each correct B or N answer.

_____ **Total Score:** Finding the Main Idea

B | Recalling Facts

How well do you remember the facts in the article? Put an X in the box next to the answer that correctly completes each statement about the article.

1. On the night of May 4, 1971, the dogs in Saint-Jean-Vianney
   - ☐ a. were unusually quiet.
   - ☐ b. ran away from the village.
   - ☐ c. barked incessantly.

2. Beneath the village's topsoil lay a
   - ☐ a. 100-foot deep layer of unstable clay.
   - ☐ b. 100-foot deep layer of sand.
   - ☐ c. flowing river.

3. On the night of May 4, most adults in the village were
   - ☐ a. sleeping.
   - ☐ b. taking a walk.
   - ☐ c. watching television.

4. When bus driver Jules Girard saw the road ahead of him sinking before his eyes, he
   - ☐ a. told his passengers to leave by the front door.
   - ☐ b. told his passengers to leave by the back door.
   - ☐ c. plunged the bus into the opening.

5. After the disaster, most of the residents
   - ☐ a. moved to a community in nearby Arvida.
   - ☐ b. chose to remain in Saint-Jean-Vianney.
   - ☐ c. moved to the city of Quebec.

Score 5 points for each correct answer.

_____ **Total Score:** Recalling Facts

C | Making Inferences

When you combine your own experience and information from a text to draw a conclusion that is not directly stated in that text, you are making an inference. Below are five statements that may or may not be inferences based on information in the article. Label the statements using the following key:

C—Correct Inference   **F—Faulty Inference**

_____ 1. There were no indications that anything was wrong in the village of Saint-Jean-Vianney before the night of May 4, 1971.

_____ 2. Saint-Jean-Vianney will be rebuilt one day.

_____ 3. Jules Girard saved the lives of the passengers on his bus.

_____ 4. Dogs can sense movement and changes beneath the surface of the earth.

_____ 5. The heavy spring rains and early thaw contributed to the disaster in Saint-Jean-Vianney.

Score 5 points for each correct answer.

_____ **Total Score:** Making Inferences

D | Using Words Precisely

Each numbered sentence below contains an underlined word or phrase from the article. Following the sentence are three definitions. One definition is closest to the meaning of the underlined word. One definition is opposite or nearly opposite. Label those two definitions using the following key. Do not label the remaining definition.

C—Closest   O—Opposite or Nearly Opposite

1. They all began sniffing the ground, running wildly in circles, and barking <u>incessantly</u>.

_____ a. ceaselessly

_____ b. loudly

_____ c. occasionally

2. When sand like this becomes <u>saturated</u> with moisture, it can cause the clay to dissolve and liquefy.

_____ a. burned

_____ b. drenched

_____ c. dried

3. When sand like this becomes saturated with moisture, it can cause the clay to dissolve and <u>liquefy</u>.

_____ a. disappear

_____ b. turn to a liquid

_____ c. turn to a solid

4. He saw that there was only a black <u>void</u> where his neighbor's house had once stood.

_____ a. crowded space

_____ b. outline

_____ c. emptiness

5. "I don't understand," Paquette cried in <u>anguish</u>.

_____ a. anger

_____ b. distress

_____ c. joy

_____ Score 3 points for each correct C answer.

_____ Score 2 points for each correct O answer.

_____ **Total Score:** Using Words Precisely

Enter the four total scores in the spaces below, and add them together to find your Reading Comprehension Score. Then record your score on the graph on page 135.

Score	Question Type	Lesson 13
_____	Finding the Main Idea	
_____	Recalling Facts	
_____	Making Inferences	
_____	Using Words Precisely	
_____	**Reading Comprehension Score**	

Author's Approach

Put an X in the box next to the correct answer.

1. The author uses the first sentence of the article to

☐ a. inform the reader that something bad is about to happen.

☐ b. convey a cheerful mood.

☐ c. express an opinion about the stupidity of the village residents.

2. From the statements below, choose those that you believe the author would agree with.

☐ a. Saint-Jean-Vianney should never have been built on the site of the landslide.

☐ b. The houses that sank into the clay were not well constructed.

☐ c. The residents of Saint-Jean-Vianney will never forget the night of the disaster.

3. In this article, "The name of Saint-Jean-Vianney disappeared from atlases and road maps" means the

☐ a. name disappeared from the map as mysteriously as the village had disappeared from the earth.

☐ b. village was too small to appear on a map.

☐ c. name was removed because the village no longer existed.

4. The author tells this story mainly by

☐ a. comparing the disaster in 1971 to more common landslides.

☐ b. telling the experiences of some of the village residents.

☐ c. telling what happened to Robert Paquette.

_____ Number of correct answers

Record your personal assessment of your work on the Critical Thinking Chart on page 136.

CRITICAL THINKING

Summarizing and Paraphrasing

Follow the directions provided for question 1. Put an X in the box next to the correct answer for question 2.

1. Reread paragraph 7 in the article. Below, write a summary of the paragraph in no more than 25 words.

_____

_____

_____

Reread your summary and decide whether it covers the important ideas in the paragraph. Next, decide how to shorten the summary to 15 words or less without leaving out any essential information. Write this summary below.

_____

_____

_____

2. Choose the sentence that correctly restates the following sentence from the article:

"One man painted the exposed part of his home's foundation, but by the following spring, the ground next to the house had sunk more than half a foot, leaving the unpainted section of the foundation exposed."

☐ a.   One man painted his house, causing the ground around it to sink.

☐ b.   About a year after one man painted the foundation of his house, the ground sank revealing even more of the foundation.

☐ c.   One man painted part of the foundation of his house and then, in the spring, uncovered and painted the rest of the foundation.

_____ Number of correct answers

Record your personal assessment of your work on the Critical Thinking Chart on page 136.

Critical Thinking

Put an X in the box next to the correct answer for questions 1, 2, and 4. Follow the directions provided for the other questions.

1. Which of the following statements from the article is an opinion rather than a fact?

☐ a.   "The village of Saint-Jean-Vianney had been built on the site of a massive landslide that had occurred 500 years earlier."

☐ b.   "The Laval house was swept away as the ground beneath it dissolved."

☐ c.   "Most of the dogs in Saint-Jean-Vianney were well-behaved."

2. From the article, you can predict that if Robert Paquette had stayed inside his home,

- ☐ a. he would have died.
- ☐ b. the rest of his family would have survived.
- ☐ c. he would have survived.

3. Choose from the letters below to correctly complete the following statement. Write the letters on the lines.

In the article, _____ and _____ are alike.

- a. the fate of Roy family members
- b. the fate of Laval family members
- c. the fate of Paquette family members

4. What was the cause of the dogs' strange behavior on the night of the disaster?

- ☐ a. One woman slapped her dog.
- ☐ b. The dogs sensed the earth shifting beneath them.
- ☐ c. The people of Saint-Jean-Vianney couldn't understand dog language.

5. Which paragraphs from the article provide evidence that supports your answer to question 3?

_____

_____ Number of correct answers

Record your personal assessment of your work on the Critical Thinking Chart on page 136.

Personal Response

What was most surprising or interesting to you about this article?

_____

_____

_____

_____

Self-Assessment

Which concepts or ideas from the article were difficult to understand?

_____

_____

_____

Which were easy to understand?

_____

_____

_____

_____

CRITICAL THINKING

THE CIRCUS TROUPE'S LAST PERFORMANCE

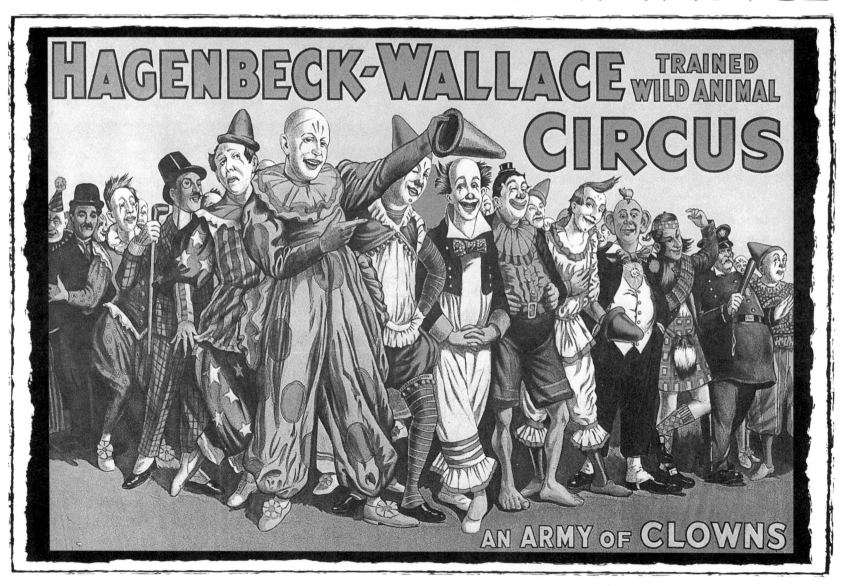

During World War I, the Hagenbeck-Wallace Circus was one of the world's largest tent shows. On the night of June 22, 1918, the show was traveling from Michigan City, Indiana, to Hammond, Indiana. The circus moved with 14 flatcars carrying tents and equipment, seven animal cars, and four sleepers for the show folk. The sleepers were old-fashioned Pullman cars, built of wood and lit by gas lamps. In the sleeping cars, which were hitched to the very end of the train, were 300 circus people: clowns, acrobats, animal trainers, jugglers, and dancers. There was Nellie Jewel, the famous animal trainer; Hercules Navarro, the strongman; and Joe Coyle, the famous clown. Coyle's family had been complaining that they missed him when he traveled with the circus. So, as a special treat, Coyle's wife and children had joined him for a while. The children were overjoyed by the double thrill of seeing their father and getting to travel on the circus train.

2   As the train sped through the night, the crew became aware of an overheated brake box and decided to fix it. The train was passing through the town of Ivanhoe, Indiana, which had a railroad yard. The circus train pulled off the main track and onto a short track used for switching. The train was so long, however, that the last four cars—the Pullman sleeper cars holding the performers—extended back onto the main track.

3   The flagman of the circus train, Ernest Trimm, wasn't the least bit worried about the four Pullmans extending out onto the main track. Trimm set emergency flares back down the tracks and checked to be sure that the automatic signal lights shone red. Even without these precautions, however, there should have been no problem. No train was due to come down the track for more than an hour—more than enough time for the circus train's crew to repair the brake box and get the train on its way.

4   What Trimm had no way of knowing was that a special train was even then approaching. World War I was responsible

This circus poster advertises the Hagenbeck-Wallace Circus, one of the world's largest tent shows during World War I.

Onlookers watch as a crane lifts the engine of the Hagenbeck-Wallace Circus train.

for troop trains moving everywhere, carrying soldiers to training camps and to ships leaving for Europe. Alonzo K. Sargent, the engineer of the troop train, was exhausted. He had been shuttling troop trains between New York and Chicago for three days. Sargent also had been suffering from a kidney ailment and had been taking pills that contained a mild painkiller.

5   On that June evening in 1918, engineer Sargent's troop train had pulled out of the station early and was rolling down the track toward Ivanhoe, Indiana. Sargent was sound asleep at the throttle. He passed through three yellow caution signals without even slowing down. Sargent's fire tender, beside him in the locomotive's cab, was bent low over the firebox, feeding the boiler. He, too, failed to see the caution signals.

6   Flagman Trimm of the circus train, was back down the track behind his train. Trimm couldn't believe his eyes as he saw the troop train bearing down toward the circus train. He watched in disbelief as the approaching locomotive ran the three caution lights. Then, Trimm's disbelief turned to horror as the troop train, without slackening its pace, passed through a red stop signal—and kept right on going. Trimm waved his red lantern frantically. Then in a last, desperate effort, he heaved it through the engineer's window of the speeding locomotive. The thrown lantern had no effect on the sleeping engineer.

7   The locomotive plowed in rapid succession through the wooden sides of the first, second, third, and fourth sleeper cars of the circus train. The wooden Pullmans shattered, and the old-fashioned gas lights started fires in the wreckage.

8   More than 85 people died, most of them as the result of burns. Fifty-three badly burned bodies, only three of them identifiable, were buried in a single mass grave. Strongman Hercules Navarro was alive but paralyzed as a result of the crash. Clown Joe Coyle lived through the accident, but his wife and children died.

9   Panic broke out among the people of the nearby town of Ivanhoe, where the people believed that wild animals had escaped from their circus cages. Rumors claimed that lions and tigers were running wild through the streets. The truth, however, was that most of the animals had been in the forward section of the train, which had not been affected by the wreck. A few animals had been killed in the crash, and police later had to destroy a few other animals that had been painfully injured.

10   Some time after the accident, engineer Sargent was brought to trial. One of the most damaging points against the engineer was the tale told by his fire tender. Right after the crash, the fire tender had run up and down the wreckage shouting, "The engineer was asleep! The engineer was asleep!" Engineer Sargent was, nevertheless, judged to be not guilty.

11   On the evening after the wreck, the circus opened on schedule. Circus performers and acts from all over the country rushed to Indiana and substituted for dead and injured performers.

12   Truckloads of flowers from show people all over the country arrived at the circus grounds. An entire vanload of blooms arrived from the great entertainer George M. Cohan. But the flower that was best remembered was a single rose. It came from a child who had seen the show just before the crash. The card that came with the flower read: "From a little girl who laughed at your show and now cries for you."

If you have been timed while reading this article, enter your reading time below. Then turn to the Words-per-Minute Table on page 133 and look up your reading speed (words per minute). Enter your reading speed on the graph on page 134.

Reading Time: Lesson 14

_____ : _____
Minutes   *Seconds*

A | Finding the Main Idea

One statement below expresses the main idea of the article. One statement is too general, or too broad. The other statement explains only part of the article; it is too narrow. Label the statements using the following key:

M—Main Idea   **B—Too Broad**   **N—Too Narrow**

_____ 1. Circus performers all over the country responded to the tragedy in Indiana.

_____ 2. Clown Joe Coyle survived the train wreck that wiped out his family.

_____ 3. A sleeping engineer ran his locomotive into a circus train, killing dozens of people.

_____ Score 15 points for a correct M answer.

_____ Score 5 points for each correct B or N answer.

_____ **Total Score:** Finding the Main Idea

B | Recalling Facts

How well do you remember the facts in the article? Put an X in the box next to the answer that correctly completes each statement about the article.

1. The circus train wreck occurred during
   ☐ a. the Civil War.
   ☐ b. World War I.
   ☐ c. World War II.

2. The circus train stopped to
   ☐ a. put on a special performance.
   ☐ b. repair a brake box.
   ☐ c. let a special troop train pass by.

3. As the oncoming locomotive passed flagman Ernest Trimm, he
   ☐ a. set out emergency flares.
   ☐ b. checked that the automatic signal lights were set red.
   ☐ c. heaved his lantern through the engineer's window.

4. Entertainer George M. Cohan
   ☐ a. rushed to Indiana and substituted for injured performers.
   ☐ b. sent an entire vanload of blooms.
   ☐ c. sent a single rose.

5. Clown Joe Coyle's family was traveling with him because his children
   ☐ a. were part of his circus act.
   ☐ b. wanted to learn to be clowns like their famous father.
   ☐ c. missed him when he was on the circus tour.

Score 5 points for each correct answer.

_____ **Total Score:** Recalling Facts

C | Making Inferences

When you combine your own experience and information from a text to draw a conclusion that is not directly stated in that text, you are making an inference. Below are five statements that may or may not be inferences based on information in the article. Label the statements using the following key:

C—Correct Inference   F—Faulty Inference

_____ 1. The flagman for the circus train was careless.

_____ 2. Engineer Alonzo Sargent should not have worked three days in a row.

_____ 3. World War I was, in part, responsible for the train wreck.

_____ 4. Fewer people would have died or been injured if the old Pullman cars had been made of steel.

_____ 5. The placement of the sleeper cars on the main track contributed to the number of dead and injured.

Score 5 points for each correct answer.

_____ **Total Score:** Making Inferences

D | Using Words Precisely

Each numbered sentence below contains an underlined word or phrase from the article. Following the sentence are three definitions. One definition is closest to the meaning of the underlined word. One definition is opposite or nearly opposite. Label those two definitions using the following key. Do not label the remaining definition.

C—Closest   O—Opposite or Nearly Opposite

1. In the sleeping cars, which were <u>hitched</u> to the very end of the train, were 300 circus people.

_____ a. fastened

_____ b. cut loose from

_____ c. passed

2. Even without these <u>precautions</u>, however, there should have been no problem.

_____ a. safeguards

_____ b. substitutes

_____ c. acts of carelessness or negligence

3. He [the engineer] had been <u>shuttling</u> troop trains between New York and Chicago for three days.

_____ a. calling

_____ b. moving back and forth

_____ c. holding in one place

4. ...the troop train, without <u>slackening</u> its pace, passed through a red stop signal.

_____ a. speeding up

_____ b. slowing down

_____ c. noticing

5. The locomotive plowed <u>in rapid succession</u> through the wooden sides of the first, second, third, and fourth sleeper cars of the circus train.

_____ a. all at once

_____ b. one after another

_____ c. strongly

_____ Score 3 points for each correct C answer.

_____ Score 2 points for each correct O answer.

_____ **Total Score:** Using Words Precisely

Enter the four total scores in the spaces below, and add them together to find your Reading Comprehension Score. Then record your score on the graph on page 135.

Score	Question Type	Lesson 14
_____	Finding the Main Idea	
_____	Recalling Facts	
_____	Making Inferences	
_____	Using Words Precisely	
_____	**Reading Comprehension Score**	

Author's Approach

Put an X in the box next to the correct answer.

1. What is the author's purpose in writing "The Circus Troupe's Last Performance"?

☐ a. To convince the reader that engineer Sargent was responsible for the train crash

☐ b. To tell the reader about the life of circus performers

☐ c. To inform the reader about a tragic train accident involving a circus troupe

2. From the statement "The thrown lantern had no effect on the sleeping engineer," you can conclude that the author wants the reader to think that the

☐ a. noise didn't wake the engineer up.

☐ b. engineer ignored the thrown lantern.

☐ c. lantern landed so far away from the engineer that he didn't notice it.

3. How is the author's purpose for writing the article expressed in paragraph 11?

☐ a. The author explains that when circus performers are hurt or killed, others must substitute for them.

☐ b. The author explains how circus performers across the country responded to the accident.

☐ c. The author suggests that, even after a tragic accident, the circus must go on as scheduled.

CRITICAL THINKING

4. The author tells this story mainly by

☐ a. telling the circumstances surrounding the accident.

☐ b. retelling personal experiences of the show people on the train.

☐ c. comparing flagman Trimm to engineer Sargent.

_____ Number of correct answers

Record your personal assessment of your work on the Critical Thinking Chart on page 136.

Summarizing and Paraphrasing

Follow the directions provided for question 1. Put an X in the box next to the correct answer for question 2.

1. Complete the following one-sentence summary of the article using the lettered phrases from the phrase bank below. Write the letters on the lines.

Phrase Bank:

a. the crash and its aftermath

b. a description of the train and its passengers

c. why the circus train stopped and the troop train was heading its way

The article about the circus train accident begins with _____, goes on to explain _____, and ends with _____.

2. Choose the sentence that correctly restates the following sentence from the article:

"Panic broke out among the people of the nearby town of Ivanhoe, where the people believed that wild animals had escaped from their circus cages."

☐ a. The people of Ivanhoe were panic-stricken because wild animals had escaped from their cages.

☐ b. The people of Ivanhoe were frightened when they saw the wild animals escape from their cages.

☐ c. People in Ivanhoe were panic-stricken because they thought that the wild animals on the train had escaped.

_____ Number of correct answers

Record your personal assessment of your work on the Critical Thinking Chart on page 136.

Critical Thinking

Follow the directions provided for questions 1, 3, 4, and 5. Put an X in the box next to the correct answer for question 2.

1. For each statement below, write O if it expresses an opinion and write F if it expresses a fact.

_____ a. Alonzo Sargent was solely responsible for the train crash.

_____ b. During World War I, the Hagenbeck-Wallace Circus was one of the world's largest tent shows.

_____ c. More than 85 people died in the train crash.

2. Judging from the fire tender's actions as told in this article, you can conclude that he thought

☐ a. Sargent had caused the accident.

☐ b. Sargent should not be blamed for the accident.

☐ c. he was partly to blame for the accident.

3. Choose from the letters below to correctly complete the following statement. Write the letters on the lines.

In the article, _____ and _____ are alike.

a. Joe Coyle's condition after the crash

b. the condition of Joe Coyle's wife and children after the crash

c. Hercules Navarro's condition after the crash

4. Read paragraph 2. Then choose from the letters below to correctly complete the following statement. Write the letters on the lines.

According to paragraph 2, _____ because _____.

a. the troop train pulled off onto a short track

b. the circus train pulled off onto a short track

c. an overheated brake needed to be fixed

5. In which paragraph did you find the information or details to answer question 3?

_____

_____ Number of correct answers

Record your personal assessment of your work on the Critical Thinking Chart on page 136.

Personal Response

Would you recommend this article to other students? Explain.

_____

_____

_____

_____

Self-Assessment

When reading the article, I was having trouble with

_____

_____

_____

_____

CRITICAL THINKING

Compare and Contrast

Think about the articles you have read in Unit Two. Pick four disasters in which luck or chance played a major role. Write the title of the articles in the first column of the chart below. Use information you learned from the articles to fill in the empty boxes in the chart.

Title	What part did luck or chance play in this disaster?	Which people involved in the disaster were luckiest? Most unlucky?	What could have been done to prevent the disaster or make it less damaging?

Of all the people involved in these disasters, I felt sorriest for _____ because _____

_____

_____

Words-per-Minute Table

Unit Two

Directions: If you were timed while reading an article, refer to the Reading Time you recorded in the box at the end of the article. Use this words-per-minute table to determine your reading speed for that article. Then plot your reading speed on the graph on page 134.

Lesson / No. of Words	8 / 1164	9 / 881	10 / 1095	11 / 786	12 / 841	13 / 954	14 / 922	Seconds
1:30	776	587	730	524	561	636	615	90
1:40	698	529	657	472	505	572	553	100
1:50	635	481	597	429	459	520	503	110
2:00	582	441	548	393	421	477	461	120
2:10	537	407	505	363	388	440	426	130
2:20	499	378	469	337	360	409	395	140
2:30	466	352	438	314	336	382	369	150
2:40	437	330	411	295	315	358	346	160
2:50	411	311	386	277	297	337	325	170
3:00	388	294	365	262	280	318	307	180
3:10	368	278	346	248	266	301	291	190
3:20	349	264	329	236	252	286	277	200
3:30	333	252	313	225	240	273	263	210
3:40	317	240	299	214	229	260	251	220
3:50	304	230	286	205	219	249	241	230
4:00	291	220	274	197	210	239	231	240
4:10	279	211	263	189	202	229	221	250
4:20	269	203	253	181	194	220	213	260
4:30	259	196	243	175	187	212	205	270
4:40	249	189	235	168	180	204	198	280
4:50	241	182	227	163	174	197	191	290
5:00	233	176	219	157	168	191	184	300
5:10	225	171	212	152	163	185	178	310
5:20	218	165	205	147	158	179	173	320
5:30	212	160	199	143	153	173	168	330
5:40	205	155	193	139	148	168	163	340
5:50	200	151	188	135	144	164	158	350
6:00	194	147	183	131	140	159	154	360
6:10	189	143	178	127	136	155	150	370
6:20	184	139	173	124	133	151	146	380
6:30	179	136	168	121	129	147	142	390
6:40	175	132	164	118	126	143	138	400
6:50	170	129	160	115	123	140	135	410
7:00	166	126	156	112	120	136	132	420
7:10	162	123	153	110	117	133	129	430
7:20	159	120	149	107	115	130	126	440
7:30	155	117	146	105	112	127	123	450
7:40	152	115	143	103	110	124	120	460
7:50	149	112	140	100	107	122	118	470
8:00	146	110	137	98	105	119	115	480

Minutes and Seconds

Plotting Your Progress: Reading Speed

Unit Two

Directions: If you were timed while reading an article, write your words-per-minute rate for that article in the box under the number of the lesson. Then plot your reading speed on the graph by putting a small X on the line directly above the number of the lesson, across from the number of words per minute you read. As you mark your speed for each lesson, graph your progress by drawing a line to connect the X's.

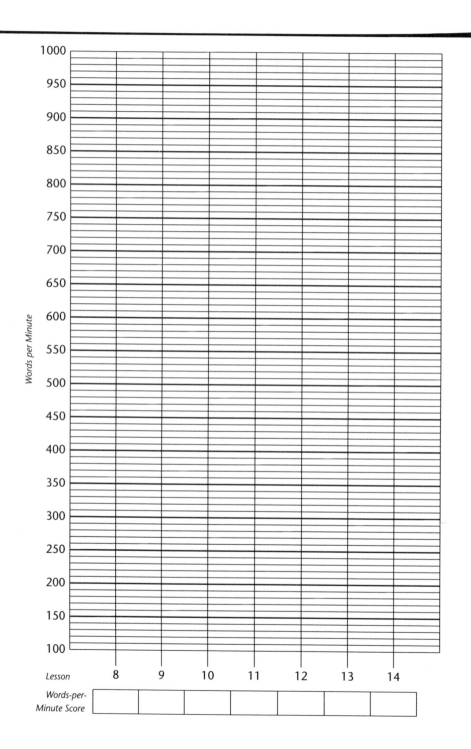

Words per Minute

Lesson	8	9	10	11	12	13	14
Words-per-Minute Score							

Plotting Your Progress: Reading Comprehension

Unit Two

Directions: Write your Reading Comprehension score for each lesson in the box under the number of the lesson. Then plot your score on the graph by putting a small X on the line directly above the number of the lesson and across from the score you earned. As you mark your score for each lesson, graph your progress by drawing a line to connect the X's.

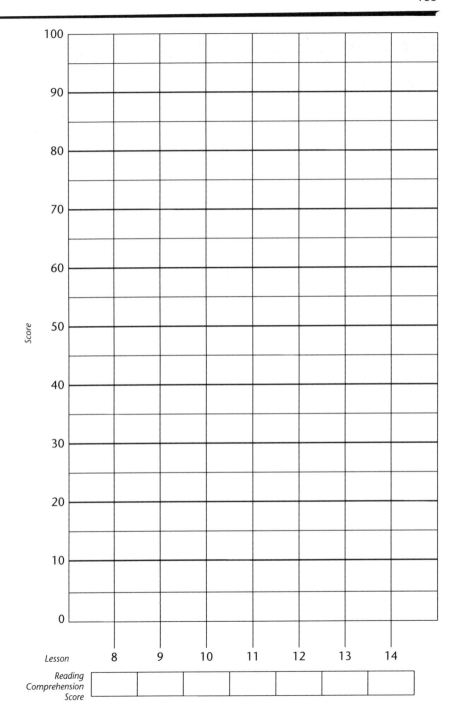

Plotting Your Progress: Critical Thinking

Unit Two

Directions: Work with your teacher to evaluate your responses to the Critical Thinking questions for each lesson. Then fill in the appropriate spaces in the chart below. For each lesson and each type of Critical Thinking question, do the following: Mark a minus sign (–) in the box to indicate areas in which you feel you could improve. Mark a plus sign (+) to indicate areas in which you feel you did well. Mark a minus-slash-plus sign (–/+) to indicate areas in which you had mixed success. Then write any comments you have about your performance, including ideas for improvement.

Lesson	Author's Approach	Summarizing and Paraphrasing	Critical Thinking
8			
9			
10			
11			
12			
13			
14			

UNIT THREE

BLACK DEATH
The End of the World

Rats were responsible for the spread of the plague. This painting, titled Dance of the Rats During Plague Time, *was painted around 1800.*

Bring out your dead! Bring out your dead!" the driver cried as the horse-drawn carts rumbled through the streets of Europe in the 1300s. Bodies were dragged from almost every house and thrown onto the carts. Corpse was tossed on top of corpse until the bodies were like logs in a pile of firewood. Sometimes several bodies were carried out of the same house. The Black Death had struck! One person in every three would die of the plague before it ran its course.

2   The Black Death was the worst calamity of all times, wiping out the entire populations of some villages. In the large city of Smolensk, Russia, only five people survived the plague. Nine out of every ten citizens of London fell victim to the Black Death. Virtually the entire populations of Iceland and Cyprus were wiped out.

3   So many people were struck down by the plague that the supply of coffins was soon exhausted, and the dead were carried on wooden planks to huge mass-burial pits. Corpses were piled several high, and then a thin layer of dirt was shoveled over them. Often the burials took place with no member of the family or clergy present. As people fled before the spreading plague, spouse abandoned spouse, and parents forsook children.

4   The plague spread quickly from person to person. People went to bed well and were dead by morning. A doctor might arrive at a home to treat a victim only to catch the plague and die before the original sufferer.

5   The Black Death derived its name from the color of the victim's skin in death; a person who was infected always died within three days, skin covered by black patches. There were other symptoms too. Patients developed egg-sized swellings in the groin and armpits. Sometimes victims coughed and sweated violently.

6   The first people to know the horror of the Black Death were the Chinese, who were hit earlier in the 14th century. The disease quickly spread to the Tartars, a people originally from the area where the present-day borders of China and the Commonwealth of Independent States (formerly the Soviet Union) meet. The Tartars, under their great leader Kipchak Janiberg, had fought their way westward across Russia. They had conquered all the Russian lands as far into Europe as the Black Sea—and they carried the plague with them.

7   The Tartar advance had been halted by a trading colony of Italians located in a city on the Black Sea. As more and more of Kipchak's Tartars became victims of the Black Death, he began to realize that the Italian city would never fall to him. Kipchak's troops had brought huge *catapults*, devices like giant slingshots, with them. The Tartars used them to throw huge stones against the stone walls of forts. Kipchak had the catapults loaded with the bodies of Tartars who had died of the Black Death. The corpses were thrown over the walls and into the city, where

People believed that one way to escape the plague was by fleeing to the country. This woodcut from 1630 shows Londoners as they leave the city for the surrounding countryside. Note the skeletons and dead body along the way.

they quickly spread the plague to the Italian colonists.

8   Both Italians and Tartars abandoned the city. Some of the Italians boarded a galley and rowed to Italy as fast as they could. When the galley arrived at the Italian port of Messina, the inhabitants of the port found some of the rowers dead and the remainder dying of the plague. The Black Death had come to Italy.

9   The plague quickly spread throughout Italy and passed on to France. From France, the plague was carried across the English Channel to Great Britain. The cycle of death was completed when the plague spread from Britain to all the rest of Europe, sparing no country. Human survival was threatened. No wonder people said,—and believed—"This is the end of the world."

10   Many people believed that the plague was caused by the wrath of God. Societies of *flagellants* formed. The societies derived their name from the whips members used to beat themselves and one another. Dressed in sackcloth and ashes, the flagellants moved from town to town, beating themselves with leather whips tipped with metal points.

11   The flagellation made as much sense as some of the other cures proposed for the plague. The crude science of the 14th century gave no idea of either the cause of the Black Death or its cure. Thinkers came up with an idea that combined astrology, geology, and superstition. Jupiter and Mars had passed very close to Earth, and the proximity of the two planets was believed to have caused cracks in the earth's crust. The cracks, they believed, permitted poisonous fumes from the earth's center to escape and cause the plague.

12   Since the scientists of the time had no idea of the plague's cause, their "cures" were nearly as horrible as the disease itself. People ate and drank concoctions of blood, goat urine, lizards, toads, and boils that had been dried and powdered. Plague victims were advised to rip open the bodies of puppies and pigeons and hold the torn flesh against their plague boils. While people were vainly trying these cures, the Black Death continued its deadly passage across Europe.

13   The real cause of the plague had been partially discovered by an Arab physician 400 years before. The physician had noted that the plague broke out only after rats had come out of their holes to die in the open air. This observation was accurate but failed to take into account one final piece needed for the puzzle's solution—fleas. The plague germs lived and multiplied in the bodies of fleas. Every rat had hundreds of fleas that lived on rats' blood and infected them with the Black Death. When the rats died of the plague, the fleas jumped onto the nearest people. It was the bite of the fleas that spread the plague germs to their human victims.

14   There were house rats in every 14th-century city, so nobody was spared. The Black Death carried off king and commoner alike. It raged back and forth over Europe, on and off, for 200 years. Then gradually, it died away. (Some people think that the real end of the plague didn't come until the London Fire of 1666. That fire destroyed most of London, along with the rats, fleas, and germs that caused the plague.)

15   Surprisingly, during all the 200 years that the plague ravaged Europe, the cure had been at hand. The germs of the Black Death can be destroyed by the application of soap and water.

If you have been timed while reading this article, enter your reading time below. Then turn to the Words-per-Minute Table on page 195 and look up your reading speed (words per minute). Enter your reading speed on the graph on page 196.

Reading Time: Lesson 15

_____ : _____
Minutes   Seconds

Finding the Main Idea

One statement below expresses the main idea of the article. One statement is too general, or too broad. The other statement explains only part of the article; it is too narrow. Label the statements using the following key:

M—Main Idea   **B—Too Broad**   **N—Too Narrow**

_____ 1. A deadly plague raced across Europe in the 14th century.

_____ 2. The Black Death, which killed millions of people in the 14th century, was spread by fleas.

_____ 3. Some people believed that the Black Death was caused by poisonous fumes escaping from the center of the earth.

_____ Score 15 points for a correct M answer.

_____ Score 5 points for each correct B or N answer.

_____ **Total Score:** Finding the Main Idea

B **Recalling Facts**

How well do you remember the facts in the article? Put an X in the box next to the answer that correctly completes each statement about the article.

1. The Black Death raged back and forth in Europe for
☐ a.   400 years.
☐ b.   200 years.
☐ c.   100 years.

2. Before the plague struck Europe, an Arab physician had noted that
☐ a.   there was a relationship between the plague and rats.
☐ b.   soap and water were effective against the plague.
☐ c.   there was no known cure for the disease.

3. The Tartar leader, Kipchak Janiberg, spread the plague by
☐ a.   bringing rats and fleas to Italy.
☐ b.   catapulting the bodies of his own men into an Italian trading colony.
☐ c.   infecting the waters of the Black Sea.

4. The Black Death got its name from the
☐ a.   Black Sea, where the Europeans first caught it.
☐ b.   color of the victim's skin.
☐ c.   Chinese, who first learned the horror of the plague.

5. The flagellants believed the plague was caused by
☐ a.   God's anger.
☐ b.   the close passage of Jupiter and Mars.
☐ c.   pigeons and puppies.

Score 5 points for each correct answer.

_____ **Total Score:** Recalling Facts

C Making Inferences

When you combine your own experience and information from a text to draw a conclusion that is not directly stated in that text, you are making an inference. Below are five statements that may or may not be inferences based on information in the article. Label the statements using the following key:

C—Correct Inference   **F—Faulty Inference**

_____ 1. The plague was particularly bad in Smolensk, Russia.

_____ 2. Although doctors couldn't cure plague victims, they did know how to protect themselves from the disease.

_____ 3. The plague takes a long time to kill its victims.

_____ 4. People infected by the disease were willing to try anything to survive.

_____ 5. European cities did not control the rat population.

Score 5 points for each correct answer.

_____ **Total Score:** Making Inferences

D Using Words Precisely

Each numbered sentence below contains an underlined word or phrase from the article. Following the sentence are three definitions. One definition is closest to the meaning of the underlined word. One definition is opposite or nearly opposite. Label those two definitions using the following key. Do not label the remaining definition.

C—Closest   **O—Opposite or Nearly Opposite**

1. One person in every three would die of the plague before it <u>ran its course</u>.

_____ a. started to occur

_____ b. spread to Europe

_____ c. came to an end

2. As people fled before the spreading plague, spouse abandoned spouse, and parents <u>forsook</u> children.

_____ a. abandoned

_____ b. killed

_____ c. kept

3. The Black Death <u>derived</u> its name from the color of the victim's skin in death....

_____ a. acquired

_____ b. questioned

_____ c. lost

4. People ate and drank <u>concoctions</u> of blood, goat urine, lizards, toads, and boils that had been dried and powdered.

_____ a. quarts

_____ b. mixtures

_____ c. separate drinks

5. The physician had <u>noted</u> that the plague broke out only after rats had come out of their holes to die in the open air.

_____ a. noticed

_____ b. ignored

_____ c. joked

_____ Score 3 points for each correct C answer.

_____ Score 2 points for each correct O answer.

_____ **Total Score:** Using Words Precisely

Enter the four total scores in the spaces below, and add them together to find your Reading Comprehension Score. Then record your score on the graph on page 197.

Score	Question Type	Lesson 15
_____	Finding the Main Idea	
_____	Recalling Facts	
_____	Making Inferences	
_____	Using Words Precisely	
_____	**Reading Comprehension Score**	

Author's Approach

Put an X in the box next to the correct answer.

1. The author uses the first sentence of the article to

☐ a. inform the reader about the Black Death.

☐ b. convey a mood of fear.

☐ c. capture the reader's attention.

2. What does the author mean by the statement "Surprisingly, during all the 200 years that the plague ravaged Europe, the cure had been at hand"?

☐ a. For 200 years, the cure had been something that was readily available to everyone.

☐ b. Just before the plague died out, scientists discovered the cure for it.

☐ c. People were surprised to find that some scientists had known the cure for the plague all along.

3. From the statement "The flagellation made as much sense as some of the other cures proposed for the plague," you can conclude that the author wants the reader to think that

☐ a. flagellation was a good way to cure the plague.

☐ b. the other proposed cures were better than flagellation.

☐ c. flagellation and the other proposed cures were useless against the plague.

4. Choose the statement below that best describes the author's position in paragraph 11.

☐ a. Science in the 14th century was not very advanced.

☐ b. Scientists in the 14th century knew more about the planets than scientists in the 20th century.

☐ c. Scientists in the 14th century understood what had caused the plague.

_____ Number of correct answers

Record your personal assessment of your work on the Critical Thinking Chart on page 198.

Summarizing and Paraphrasing

Put an X in the box next to the correct answer.

1. Below are summaries of the article. Choose the summary that says all the most important things about the article but in the fewest words.

☐ a. The Black Death was the worst calamity of all time. In the 1300s, one person of every three died of it. The plague began in China and quickly spread to Europe. Many people believed that the plague meant the world was about to end; no cure for the disease could be found. The plague, which was carried by fleas on rats, raged on for 200 years until it finally died away.

☐ b. Beginning in the 1300s and lasting about 200 years, the Black Death raged throughout Europe where it killed one person of every three. Scientists in the 14th century could not discover the cause of the plague or its cure. Today we know that the plague was spread by fleas and that soap and water can destroy its germs.

☐ c. The Black Death began in China and spread to Europe where it proved to be the worst calamity of all times.

2. Read the statement about the article below. Then read the paraphrase of that statement. Choose the reason that best tells why the paraphrase does not say the same thing as the statement.

Statement: The flagellants believed that the plague was caused by the wrath of God, and so they continually beat themselves and one another to try to satisfy God and seek forgiveness for their sins.

Paraphrase: Because the flagellants beat themselves and each other, they constantly asked God to forgive them.

☐ a. Paraphrase says too much.

☐ b. Paraphrase doesn't say enough.

☐ c. Paraphrase doesn't agree with the statement about the article.

_____ Number of correct answers

Record your personal assessment of your work on the Critical Thinking Chart on page 198.

Critical Thinking

Put an X in the box next to the correct answer for questions 1, 2, and 4. Follow the directions provided for question 3.

1. Which of the following statements from the article is an opinion rather than a fact?

☐ a. "The Black Death was the worst calamity of all times...."

☐ b. "In the large city of Smolensk, Russia, only five people survived the plague."

☐ c. "The Black Death derived its name from the color of the victim's skin in death; a person who was infected always died within three days, skin covered by black patches."

2. From the article, you can predict that if Europeans in the 14th century had been cleaner,

☐ a. the Black Death would have been stopped sooner.

☐ b. there would have been just as many deaths from the Black Death.

☐ c. scientists would have quickly discovered a cure for the Black Death.

3. Choose from the letters below to correctly complete the following statement. Write the letters on the lines.

According to the article, _____ caused _____, and the effect was _____.

a. a battle between Italian colonists and Tartars

b. they carried the Black Death to Italy

c. the plague to be spread to the colonists

4. What did you have to do to answer question 1?

☐ a. make a prediction (what might happen next)

☐ b. find an opinion (what someone thinks about something)

☐ c. draw a conclusion (a sensible statement based on the text and your experience)

_____ Number of correct answers

Record your personal assessment of your work on the Critical Thinking Chart on page 198.

Personal Response

What new question do you have about this topic?

_____

_____

_____

_____

Self-Assessment

From reading this article, I have learned

_____

_____

_____

_____

CRITICAL THINKING

THE GREAT CHICAGO FIRE

There is an old song about how Mrs. O'Leary's cow started the Chicago Fire. It's almost certainly not true, but for about 125 years everyone believed it. According to legend—and the song—it was Daisy the cow who started the fire by accidentally kicking over a kerosene lantern.

2   Today we know the real villain was probably Daniel "Peg Leg" Sullivan, who lived down an alley from the O'Learys. It was Sullivan who claimed he saw Daisy kick over the lantern. According to a 1997 report written by Richard Bales, however, Sullivan lied. Bales proved that a high fence blocked Sullivan's view of the O'Learys' barn. So Sullivan could not possibly have seen Daisy. Bales believes it was Sullivan who started the fire in the barn, probably from his pipe ashes, and then pinned the blame on poor Daisy. In any event, one thing is certain: the Great Chicago Fire was one of the biggest and worst human-made disasters in North American history.

3   In 1871, Patrick and Catherine O'Leary lived on Chicago's West Side. Patrick made a poor living carrying heavy loads by hand. Catherine added to their income with a dairy business of her own. She kept five cows in the barn behind their house and sold their milk to other families in the neighborhood.

4   Late in the evening of October 8, 1871, a fire broke out in the O'Leary barn. Bales says that some of the O'Learys' tenants

were having a party that night. Sullivan crashed the party and then, half-drunk, went out to the barn to get more to drink. There, Sullivan either kicked over the lantern himself or dropped some pipe ash on the dry hay that was scattered about. He managed to get out alive, but many others were not so lucky.

5   The Chicago Fire turned deadly not only because of Sullivan's carelessness but also because of the way Chicago itself was built and managed. The city had 651 miles of wooden sidewalks. There were 60,000 buildings—most of them constructed of wood. In the midst of all this wood, the fire department had 17 horse-drawn steam pumpers and 18 hook-and-ladder trucks. Although Chicago had a population of 350,000, the fire department had a force of only 200.

6   The night the Great Fire broke out, Chicago's firefighters were dead tired. They had faced 30 fires during the week before, and the last fire had been an especially bad one. The firefighters had drunk a lot of whiskey after that blaze, and many of them had hangovers. Later, some critics were to claim that many firefighters were still drunk when the big fire broke out.

7   The fire department's central head-quarters was located in the city's stone "fireproof" courthouse. A fire lookout atop the courthouse's tall tower spotted smoke from the fire at the O'Leary barn and sent in the alarm. Unfortunately, the lookout reported the wrong location. By the time the correct location was discovered, the fire had gotten a solid start. The

fire spread out of control, forcing citizens to flee their homes and driving everyone, including the fire department, before it. The firefighters fought back bravely, but they had little to fight with.

8   The wooden buildings and sidewalks gave off millions of flying sparks, some of them the size of baseballs. And the winds resulting from the fires drove those fire-balls as far as well-hit baseballs. The fireballs crossed streets and jumped over buildings and across the river, spreading the blaze.

9   The fire raged on. Racing before it were the looters, drunk with liquor from the

People flee along Chicago's Michigan Avenue as the great fire rages.

Schock, Bigford and Co. was the first store to reopen in the burned-out business district.

saloons and stores they'd broken into. Merchants and homeowners who tried to protect their possessions were struck down—even killed. The fire moved toward Chicago's "fireproof" courthouse. Although the building was faced with a layer of limestone and its interior was marble, the heat of the fire was too intense, even for stone, and the courthouse started to go. The basement of the building housed the city's jail, where dozens of prisoners were locked up and screaming to be released. A police captain ordered the police to take the murderers outside and keep them under guard there. All other prisoners were freed.

10   The convicts ran down the street, unable to believe their good fortune. Their fortune really improved when they reached a well-known jewelry store. The store was already smoldering. The store's owner held out his hands to the convicts. In them he held rings, necklaces, and bracelets. "Help yourselves, gentlemen," he called. The jeweler realized that if the convicts didn't get the goods, the fire would. It made little difference to him whether the jewelry was stolen by convicts or melted by the fire. The jeweler, A.H. Miller, picked out a few of his most valuable gems and walked away with them.

11   People trapped in the second and third floors of houses with bottom floors on fire threw their most precious possessions to others gathered in the street. One woman dropped a large bundle of bedsheets to a man waiting below her windows. The woman quickly followed her belongings through the window, when she saw the man run off with the bundle. The bundle contained the woman's baby. The screaming mother pursued the thief as he cut in and out among the crowd, fleeing across a bridge leading from the burning city. Thief and bundle disappeared in the mass of people. The heartsick mother was thinking of leaping to her death over the railing of the bridge when she spotted her baby. He was alive, lying on some bales of cotton 10 feet below. The mother climbed down the bridge's steelwork and retrieved her infant.

12   The rest of Chicago did not get off so luckily. Its doom was sealed by a single burning plank carried aloft by the powerful, hot winds stirred up by the blaze. The burning plank sailed through the air until it reached the waterworks, where it crashed through the wooden roof. The waterworks had been considered fireproof, but its wooden ceiling was soon on fire. The ceiling fell onto the pumps that supplied the city with water and put them out of action. The firefighters, left without water, were forced to give up the battle.

13   The fire burned out of control for 30 hours, until the early morning of October 10, 1871. Then the wind died down, and it started to rain. The rain was soon spattering onto the cinders and charred wreckage of what had been the city of Chicago. The fire destroyed $200 million worth of buildings and left 100,000 people homeless.

14   Chicagoans, believing Sullivan, turned their wrath on Patrick O'Leary. O'Leary, fearing for his life, escaped by dressing as a woman. He hid at a friend's house until the mob's anger died.

15   Chicago made a fast recovery from the fire. Six months after the blaze, half of the city had been rebuilt. In just a few years there was no sign of the fire, and the population had doubled. Hundreds of the city's new citizens were happy to buy a dramatic souvenir of the Great Fire. Many of Chicago's old-timers had discovered that they could make money selling the hoof of the cow that supposedly kicked over the lantern and started the fire. They sold hundreds of that hoof. But the cow has had the last laugh. In 1997, the Chicago City Council voted to clear Daisy and the O'Learys of all arson charges.

If you have been timed while reading this article, enter your reading time below. Then turn to the Words-per-Minute Table on page 195 and look up your reading speed (words per minute). Enter your reading speed on the graph on page 196.

Reading Time: Lesson 16

_____ : _____
Minutes   Seconds

A | Finding the Main Idea

One statement below expresses the main idea of the article. One statement is too general, or too broad. The other statement explains only part of the article; it is too narrow. Label the statements using the following key:

M—Main Idea　　　　**B—Too Broad**　　　　**N—Too Narrow**

_____ 1. Thousands of people were left homeless when fire destroyed 19th-century Chicago.

_____ 2. A big fire started in the O'Leary barn on Chicago's West Side when Daniel Sullivan scattered pipe ash on dry hay.

_____ 3. Chicago was the scene of one of the greatest human-made disasters in North America.

_____ Score 15 points for a correct M answer.

_____ Score 5 points for each correct B or N answer.

_____ **Total Score:** Finding the Main Idea

B | Recalling Facts

How well do you remember the facts in the article? Put an X in the box next to the answer that correctly completes each statement about the article.

1. Daniel Sullivan went into the O'Learys' barn to
   - ☐ a. steal Daisy the cow.
   - ☐ b. get more drinks for a party.
   - ☐ c. smoke.

2. A fire spotter, whose job was to report fires,
   - ☐ a. was asleep at his post.
   - ☐ b. panicked and couldn't send the alarm.
   - ☐ c. reported the wrong location of the fire.

3. Some sparks from the fire were as large as
   - ☐ a. basketballs.
   - ☐ b. soccer balls.
   - ☐ c. baseballs.

4. Prisoners, except for murderers, were
   - ☐ a. sent to another jail.
   - ☐ b. freed.
   - ☐ c. put to work fighting the fire.

5. The fire was finally put out
   - ☐ a. with the help of fire departments from other cities.
   - ☐ b. when it started to rain.
   - ☐ c. when all the wood in the city had burned.

Score 5 points for each correct answer.

_____ **Total Score:** Recalling Facts

C | Making Inferences

When you combine your own experience and information from a text to draw a conclusion that is not directly stated in that text, you are making an inference. Below are five statements that may or may not be inferences based on information in the article. Label the statements using the following key:

C—Correct Inference   F—Faulty Inference

_____ 1. Daniel Sullivan blamed Daisy to protect himself.

_____ 2. If Chicago had had concrete sidewalks, the fire may not have spread as fast.

_____ 3. Jeweler A.H. Miller was not a very practical man.

_____ 4. Whoever designed the "fireproof" waterworks probably didn't expect a fire to start on the ceiling.

_____ 5. The people who sold souvenir hooves of the O'Learys' cow were swindlers.

Score 5 points for each correct answer.

_____ **Total Score:** Making Inferences

D | Using Words Precisely

Each numbered sentence below contains an underlined word or phrase from the article. Following the sentence are three definitions. One definition is closest to the meaning of the underlined word. One definition is opposite or nearly opposite. Label those two definitions using the following key. Do not label the remaining definition.

C—Closest   O—Opposite or Nearly Opposite

1. The store was already smoldering.

_____ a. burning slowly without flame

_____ b. burning out of control

_____ c. being looted

2. The screaming mother pursued the thief as he cut in and out among the crowd....

_____ a. avoided

_____ b. chased

_____ c. stabbed

3. The mother climbed down the bridge's steelwork and retrieved her infant.

_____ a. recovered

_____ b. lost

_____ c. punished

4. Chicagoans, believing Sullivan, turned their wrath on Patrick O'Leary.

_____ a. attention

_____ b. rage

_____ c. calmness

5. He hid at a friend's house until the <u>mob</u>'s anger died.

_____ a. disorderly crowd

_____ b. crowd of firefighters

_____ c. well-behaved crowd

_____ Score 3 points for each correct C answer.

_____ Score 2 points for each correct O answer.

_____ **Total Score:** Using Words Precisely

Enter the four total scores in the spaces below, and add them together to find your Reading Comprehension Score. Then record your score on the graph on page 197.

Score	Question Type	Lesson 16
_____	Finding the Main Idea	
_____	Recalling Facts	
_____	Making Inferences	
_____	Using Words Precisely	
_____	**Reading Comprehension Score**	

Author's Approach

Put an X in the box next to the correct answer.

1. What does the author mean by the statement "Sullivan crashed the party and then, half-drunk, went out to the barn to get more to drink"?

☐ a. Sullivan, who had not been invited to the party, unsteadily went to the barn looking for more to drink.

☐ b. Sullivan fell down at the party because he had already had a lot to drink.

☐ c. Half-drunk, Sullivan broke up the party and then went out to the barn for more to drink.

2. What is the author's purpose in writing "The Great Chicago Fire"?

☐ a. To convince the reader that Daniel Sullivan was responsible for the fire

☐ b. To tell the reader about the causes and effects of the fire

☐ c. To express an opinion about the people who looted and robbed during the fire

3. Choose the statement below that is the weakest argument for believing that Daisy the cow was to blame for the Chicago Fire.

☐ a. Daniel Sullivan claimed he saw Daisy kick over the lantern.

☐ b. Many old-timers claimed that they had the hooves of the cow that started the fire.

☐ c. In 1997, the Chicago City Council cleared Daisy and the O'Learys of all arson charges.

4. What does the author imply by saying "Chicagoans, believing Sullivan, turned their wrath on Patrick O'Leary"?

☐ a. Chicagoans blamed Sullivan for the fire and wanted to hurt him.

☐ b. O'Leary blamed Sullivan for the fire and wanted to hurt him.

☐ c. Chicagoans blamed O'Leary for the fire and wanted to hurt him.

_____ Number of correct answers

Record your personal assessment of your work on the Critical Thinking Chart on page 198.

Paraphrase: For about 125 years everyone believed that Daisy the cow started the Great Chicago Fire by kicking over a lantern, but today most people think that Daniel Sullivan was to blame for the blaze.

☐ a. Paraphrase says too much.

☐ b. Paraphrase doesn't say enough.

☐ c. Paraphrase doesn't agree with the statement about the article.

_____ Number of correct answers

Record your personal assessment of your work on the Critical Thinking Chart on page 198.

Summarizing and Paraphrasing

Follow the directions provided for question 1. Put an X in the box next to the correct answer for question 2.

1. Look for the important ideas and events in paragraphs 9 and 10. Summarize those paragraphs in one or two sentences.

_____

_____

_____

2. Read the statement about the article below. Then read the paraphrase of that statement. Choose the reason that best tells why the paraphrase does not say the same thing as the statement.

Statement: For many years, people have blamed the O'Learys' cow Daisy for starting the Great Chicago Fire, but in 1997 the animal's name was cleared.

Critical Thinking

Put an X in the box next to the correct answer for questions 1, 2, 4, and 5. Follow the directions provided for question 3.

1. Which of the following statements from the article is an opinion rather than a fact?

☐ a. "...the Great Chicago Fire was the biggest and worst human-made disaster in North American history."

☐ b. "Although Chicago had a population of 350,000, the fire department had a force of only 200."

☐ c. "Late in the evening of October 8, 1871, a fire broke out in the O'Leary barn."

2. Judging from the actions of the man who ran off with a woman's bedsheets, you can predict that he

☐ a. wanted to kidnap her baby.

☐ b. was only trying to help her.

☐ c. wanted only her valuables, not her child.

3. Choose from the letters below to correctly complete the following statement. Write the letters on the lines.

   On the positive side, _____, but on the negative side _____.

   a.   the fire left thousands homeless

   b.   Patrick O'Leary hid from the angry mob

   c.   Chicago made a quick recovery from the fire

4. What was the cause of the prisoners' release from jail?

   ☐ a.   They ran down the street, unable to believe their good fortune.

   ☐ b.   The owner of a jewelry store gave them his goods.

   ☐ c.   The courthouse, which housed the city's jail, was on fire.

5. If you were a city planner, how could you use the information in the article to design a town?

   ☐ a.   Make sure the sidewalks are made of concrete and the buildings are made of steel.

   ☐ b.   Make sure the sidewalks and buildings are made of wood.

   ☐ c.   Make sure the fire department maintains a small force of firefighters.

   _____ Number of correct answers

   Record your personal assessment of your work on the Critical Thinking Chart on page 198.

Personal Response

If I were the author, I would add

_____

_____

_____

because

_____

_____

_____

_____

Self-Assessment

While reading the article, I found it easiest to

_____

_____

_____

_____

DEATH ON THE MISSISSIPPI

The gaunt, worn-out men in faded blue uniforms just wanted to go home. They had been prisoners of war during the American Civil War, which had ended two weeks earlier. Now, on April 25, 1865, these Union men boarded the steamship *Sultana* in Vicksburg, Mississippi. They would get off when the ship reached Cairo, Illinois. Although weak from their prison ordeal, many of the men danced and sang as they boarded the ship.

2   The *Sultana* was a coal-burning side-wheeler with two huge twin smokestacks. It had been built in 1863. For the past two years, it had made runs on the Mississippi River between New Orleans and St. Louis. Its cargo included cotton, sugar, and live-stock. It had also ferried Union soldiers up and down the river. The *Sultana's* license allowed it to carry 376 people, including a crew of 85.

3   On April 21, the *Sultana* left New Orleans with 75 passengers and a full crew. Captain Cass Mason was in com-mand. Three days later, the steamer stopped in Vicksburg. The ship's engineer noticed that the steam boilers were leaking. A repair crew quickly fixed the boilers. Meanwhile, hundreds of happy ex-prisoners piled onto the ship. Port offi-cials, seeing the men's excitement, decided not to take the usual roll call. So no one knew the exact number of former pris-oners of war who boarded the ship. The best guess is somewhere between 1,800 and 2,000. A few more passengers and two units of Northern soldiers also boarded. In all, there were roughly 2,300 people on board the *Sultana* when its lines were cast off. That was about six times as many people as the steamer was built to carry.

4   The ship made slow progress under its great load. Speed was also hampered by the fact that the *Sultana* was sailing upriver against a current made strong by spring floods. Still, the *Sultana* made it to Memphis, Tennessee, by the evening of April 26. Again, however, the boilers acted up and needed to be repaired. A few passengers got off, and some sugar was unloaded. Also, some soldiers disembarked to explore the local sights. Several were enjoying themselves so much that they didn't make it back to the *Sultana* in time. Close to midnight, the steamer sailed on without them.

5   The *Sultana* struggled slowly up the Mississippi against the current. By 2 A.M. on April 27, the ship had gone only a few miles north of Memphis. The strain of the massive weight was affecting the boilers. Once again they began to leak, and the crew did what they could to repair them.

6   Then it happened. All of a sudden, the boilers erupted in a mammoth explosion, nearly splitting the *Sultana* in half. Hundreds of the ship's passengers were killed instantly by the blast. Hundreds more were tossed into the icy Mississippi. Many of the half-starved former prisoners either didn't know how to swim or were too weak to try. They quickly drowned.

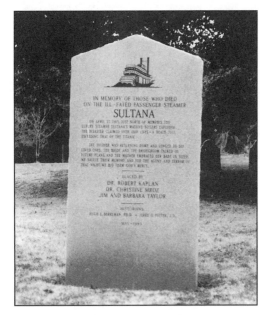

This monument to the victims of the Sultana *disaster stands in Elmwood Cemetery in Memphis, Tennessee.*

The Sultana, *loaded with passengers, steams up the Mississippi River.*

Meanwhile, hundreds of others were trapped below deck. Most died in the raging fire caused when the red-hot coals spewed out of the boilers. Even those who were not killed were badly scalded by water from the boilers.

7   Those who survived the initial blast faced a grim choice: the fire or the water. Some of the men still on board jumped into the water. Even if they couldn't swim, they thought, the water was better than the flames. One survivor later wrote, "I could see men jumping from all parts of the boat into the water, until it seemed black with men, their heads bobbing up like corks, and then disappearing beneath the turbulent waters, never to appear again."

8   Daniel McLeod, a veteran crippled at the battle of Shiloh, preferred a watery grave. He had been reading at a table in a cabin when the *Sultana* exploded. The blast sent him flying against the wall of his cabin. He was badly injured, with cuts, bruises, and burns all over his body. Both his ankles were broken and bleeding badly. McLeod used his suspenders to apply tourniquets to both legs to keep from bleeding to death. Then he spotted an army officer nearby and asked, "Captain, will you please help me?" The captain didn't know what to do. McLeod pleaded, "Throw me in the river is all I

ask. I'll burn to death here." The captain, with help from another man, lifted McLeod up and dropped him over the railing. McLeod was never seen again.

9   Not everyone died. Some managed to hang onto sections of the stern or the bow where the fire had not yet reached. A few lucky soldiers in the river grabbed pieces of drifting wreckage which kept them afloat. One man, while still on the *Sultana*, came across a heavy wooden cage with an alligator inside. He used his bayonet to kill the reptile, then rolled the cage over the side and jumped in after it. He clung to the cage until he was rescued. Those men who were strong enough ripped doors or wooden window blinds from their fastenings and used them as life preservers in the river.

10   Meanwhile, the *Sultana* drifted helplessly down the river until at last it struck a small island. Those men who were still alive jumped off the ship and scrambled desperately for shore. There they watched what was left of the flaming ship as it sank beneath the surface.

11   Rescuers came with the rising sun. Arriving in small boats, they found hundreds of half-dead men dotting both sides of the river for mile after mile. These men had survived by clinging to logs, barrels, sections of railing, doors, and

other pieces of wood. Most were burned and scalded; some had no clothes.

12   The final death toll—which included Captain Mason—was about 1,700. That made it one of the worst maritime disasters in world history. More people died on the *Sultana* than on the *Titanic* (1,503) or on the *Lusitania* (1,198). Yet it barely made it into the newspapers of the day. The papers devoted most of their coverage to the death of President Abraham Lincoln and the procession of his funeral train. The *Sultana* explosion didn't make it into many history books either. To this day, it remains one of the great, little-known tragedies in American history.

If you have been timed while reading this article, enter your reading time below. Then turn to the Words-per-Minute Table on page 195 and look up your reading speed (words per minute). Enter your reading speed on the graph on page 196.

Reading Time: Lesson 17

_____ : _____
Minutes   Seconds

A Finding the Main Idea

One statement below expresses the main idea of the article. One statement is too general, or too broad. The other statement explains only part of the article; it is too narrow. Label the statements using the following key:

M—Main Idea   **B—Too Broad**   **N—Too Narrow**

_____ 1. In 1865, the steamship *Sultana* exploded on the Mississippi River, killing most of the just-released prisoners of war on board.

_____ 2. Many of the former prisoners drowned because they didn't have the strength to swim.

_____ 3. The *Sultana* disaster is a little-known tragedy in American history.

_____ Score 15 points for a correct M answer.

_____ Score 5 points for each correct B or N answer.

_____ **Total Score:** Finding the Main Idea

B Recalling Facts

How well do you remember the facts in the article? Put an X in the box next to the answer that correctly completes each statement about the article.

1. The *Sultana's* license allowed the steamship to carry
   ☐ a. 75 people.
   ☐ b. 376 people.
   ☐ c. 2,300 people.

2. A few soldiers disembarked in Memphis and didn't return to the ship because they
   ☐ a. were enjoying themselves.
   ☐ b. were unloading sugar.
   ☐ c. saw that the boilers needed to be repaired.

3. Most of the passengers trapped below deck
   ☐ a. drowned in the icy Mississippi.
   ☐ b. were badly scalded by water from the boilers.
   ☐ c. died in the fire spread by the red-hot coals.

4. Daniel McLeod asked the ship's captain to
   ☐ a. help him kill an alligator.
   ☐ b. throw him in the river.
   ☐ c. apply tourniquets to his legs.

5. On the day of the *Sultana* explosion, the newspapers devoted most of their coverage to
   ☐ a. the sinking of the *Titanic*.
   ☐ b. the sinking of the *Lusitania*.
   ☐ c. the death and funeral of President Abraham Lincoln.

Score 5 points for each correct answer.

_____ **Total Score:** Recalling Facts

Making Inferences

When you combine your own experience and information from a text to draw a conclusion that is not directly stated in that text, you are making an inference. Below are five statements that may or may not be inferences based on information in the article. Label the statements using the following key:

C—Correct Inference   F—Faulty Inference

_____ 1. More soldiers than usual wanted to board the *Sultana* because the war had just ended.

_____ 2. *Sultana's* unusually heavy load put a strain on the steamship's boilers, which led to the explosion.

_____ 3. Port officials considered the passengers' safety before the ship left Vicksburg.

_____ 4. Daniel McLeod drowned in the Mississippi River.

_____ 5. The explosion of the *Sultana* was part of a plot to kill Union soldiers.

Score 5 points for each correct answer.

_____ **Total Score:** Making Inferences

D **Using Words Precisely**

Each numbered sentence below contains an underlined word or phrase from the article. Following the sentence are three definitions. One definition is closest to the meaning of the underlined word. One definition is opposite or nearly opposite. Label those two definitions using the following key. Do not label the remaining definition.

C—Closest   O—Opposite or Nearly Opposite

1. The <u>gaunt</u>, worn-out men in faded blue uniforms just wanted to go home.

_____ a. tall

_____ b. stout

_____ c. thin

2. Speed was also <u>hampered</u> by the fact that the *Sultana* was sailing upriver against a current made strong by spring floods.

_____ a. hindered

_____ b. measured

_____ c. assisted

3. Also, some soldiers <u>disembarked</u> to explore the local sights.

_____ a. got off

_____ b. boarded

_____ c. requested

4. All of a sudden, the boilers erupted in a <u>mammoth</u> explosion, nearly splitting the *Sultana* in half.

_____ a. insignificant

_____ b. tremendous

_____ c. deadly

5. One survivor later wrote, "I could see men jumping from all parts of the boat into the water, until it seemed black with men, their heads bobbing up like corks, and then disappearing beneath the turbulent waters, never to appear again."

_____ a. calm

_____ b. murky

_____ c. violent

_____ Score 3 points for each correct C answer.

_____ Score 2 points for each correct O answer.

_____ **Total Score:** Using Words Precisely

Enter the four total scores in the spaces below, and add them together to find your Reading Comprehension Score. Then record your score on the graph on page 197.

Score	Question Type	Lesson 17
_____	Finding the Main Idea	
_____	Recalling Facts	
_____	Making Inferences	
_____	Using Words Precisely	
_____	**Reading Comprehension Score**	

Author's Approach

Put an X in the box next to the correct answer.

1. What does the author mean by the statement "Those who survived the initial blast faced a grim choice: the fire or the water"?

☐ a. Survivors had to decide whether to take their chances by staying on board the ship or jumping into the river.

☐ b. Survivors had to decide whether they would save themselves or try to save others.

☐ c. Survivors had to choose between fighting the fire or bailing water out of the ship.

2. The main purpose of the first paragraph is to

☐ a. inform the reader about the Civil War.

☐ b. inform the reader about the *Sultana* and the men who boarded it in Vicksburg.

☐ c. inform the reader about the steamship's destination.

3. From the statement "Daniel McLeod, a veteran crippled at the battle of Shiloh, preferred a watery grave," you can conclude that the author wants the reader to think that McLeod

☐ a. had planned to kill himself when he boarded the ship.

☐ b. wanted to decide for himself how he would die.

☐ c. was a coward.

4. Choose the statement below that best describes the author's position in paragraph 12.

☐ a. The *Sultana* explosion deserves to be more widely known.

☐ b. The *Sultana* explosion was an unimportant incident.

☐ c. The entire country mourned when President Lincoln died.

_____ Number of correct answers

Record your personal assessment of your work on the Critical Thinking Chart on page 198.

Summarizing and Paraphrasing

Put an X in the box next to the correct answer.

1. Below are summaries of the article. Choose the summary that says all the most important things about the article but in the fewest words.

☐ a. Shortly after the Civil War ended, the *Sultana* exploded, but the incident received little coverage in the press.

☐ b. When the boilers on the steamship *Sultana* exploded, hundreds of people were killed instantly by the blast or died in the resulting fire. Many others drowned in the Mississippi River. Some of the survivors clung to pieces of wood until they were eventually rescued.

☐ c. Two weeks after the Civil War ended, the steamship *Sultana* exploded while traveling up the Mississippi. Although an estimated 1,700 people died in the disaster, the incident received little press coverage and remains a little-known tragedy.

2. Read the statement about the article below. Then read the paraphrase of that statement. Choose the reason that best tells why the paraphrase does not say the same thing as the statement.

Statement: When one man on board the *Sultana* came across an alligator in a wooden cage, he killed the animal, threw the cage overboard, and jumped in after it so that he could use the cage as a large life preserver.

Paraphrase: One man from the *Sultana* clung to a wooden cage he had thrown overboard.

☐ a. Paraphrase says too much.

☐ b. Paraphrase doesn't say enough.

☐ c. Paraphrase doesn't agree with the statement about the article.

_____ Number of correct answers

Record your personal assessment of your work on the Critical Thinking Chart on page 198.

Critical Thinking

Follow the directions provided for questions 1, 3, and 4. Put an X in the box next to the correct answer for the other questions.

1. For each statement below, write O if it expresses an opinion and write F if it expresses a fact.

_____ a. President Lincoln's funeral was a more important event than the *Sultana* disaster.

_____ b. The *Sultana* was carrying far more people than it was equipped to handle.

_____ c. More people died in the *Sultana* disaster than in the sinking of the *Titanic* or *Lusitania*.

2. From the information in paragraph 4, you can predict that if the soldiers had made it back to the *Sultana*,

☐ a. they would probably have died in the explosion.

☐ b. the ship wouldn't have exploded.

☐ c. the ship would have remained in Memphis.

3. Choose from the letters below to correctly complete the following statement. Write the letters on the lines.

In the article, _____ and _____ are different.

a. the fate of Captain Cass Mason

b. the fate of Daniel McLeod

c. the fate of the men who disembarked in Memphis

4. Read paragraph 6. Then choose from the letters below to correctly complete the following statement. Write the letters on the lines.

According to paragraph 6, _____ because _____.

a. hundreds of passengers were trapped below deck

b. they couldn't swim or were too tired to try

c. many of the former prisoners tossed into the river drowned

5. What did you have to do to answer question 3?

☐ a. find a contrast (how things are different)

☐ b. find a cause (why something happened)

☐ c. find a definition (what something means)

_____ Number of correct answers

Record your personal assessment of your work on the Critical Thinking Chart on page 198.

Personal Response

A question I would like answered by Captain Mason is

Self-Assessment

From reading this article, I have learned

THE BEIRUT BOMBING
Deadly Terrorist Attack

They came as peacekeepers. With the best of intentions, the men of America's Eighth Marine Battalion came to Beirut, Lebanon, as part of an international military force. Their task was to keep the peace among Lebanon's various feuding factions and to protect citizens. Marines are trained to be warriors. But in this case, they were not supposed to fight. They weren't even supposed to look as though they would fight if challenged.

2 The Marines had the additional job of guarding the airport and keeping it open to traffic. That assingment put them in a vulnerable location. Airports are flat, wide-open places, not easily defended. Worse, the Beirut airport is surrounded by mountains. Any enemy located in the nearby hills would have a huge advantage over the exposed Marines down at the airport.

3 The peacekeeping Marines were not allowed to dig in and hunker down in secure bunkers, either. Instead, they lived in the Aviation Safety Building on the edge of the airport. Although the four-

Marines and rescue personnel sift through the rubble of the Aviation Safety Building at the Beirut airport where 241 U.S. Marines were killed.

story building had guard posts, sandbags, and other barriers, these safeguards were not nearly enough to stop a determined attacker. The Marines were, in short, sitting ducks if an enemy wanted to strike.

4   The city of Beirut was no place for sitting ducks in 1983. Lebanon had been racked by religious and ethnic strife for years. A civil war had been raging since 1975. Various groups of Christians and Muslims were at each others' throats. To make matters worse, Lebanon was a pawn in the much larger game of Middle East politics. The struggle to control Lebanon involved Israel on the one hand and its old Arab enemies, such as Syria, on the other.

5   Into this tinderbox the U.S. government sent the Eighth Marine Battalion. The Marines made a tempting target for those who hated Americans. In the end, it proved to be too tempting. Snipers killed a total of six Marines who were patrolling the lawless streets of Beirut. But that wasn't enough for one terrorist group. Authorities believe that the Hezbollah, a terrorist organization supported by the government of Iran, planned an attack that would kill as many Marines as possible.

6   The terrorists picked a Sunday morning when they knew that most of the Marines would be asleep. At 6:20 A.M.

on October 23, 1983, a Mercedes truck approached the Marine barracks. The driver was a suicide bomber. His truck was filled with 5,000 pounds of highly explosive TNT. A guard noticed the suspicious-looking truck. But before the guard could stop the truck or sound the alarm, the driver floored his gas pedal. The truck roared forward, plowing through a sandbag barrier. It surged through another barrier and into the glass lobby of the building. The bomber then detonated his deadly cargo. It exploded with a deafening roar, destroying the building. The blast left a crater 30 feet deep and 40 feet wide. "I was sleeping, then suddenly I saw fire and stuff coming down all around me," said a Marine who survived. "It was like a big nightmare."

7   Meanwhile, a second truck loaded with explosives rammed into a barracks filled with French soldiers. This blast was so powerful that it moved the building 30 feet. French defense minister Charles Hernu called the bombing "an odious and cowardly attack." It killed 58 French paratroopers.

8   The death toll at the American barracks would be much higher. At first, no one knew how many Marines had died. The number kept climbing as more and more bodies were hauled out of the rubble

and lined up along the runway. It took a few days before the official death count was known. A total of 241 Marines had been killed by the terrorists.

9   Marine Major Robert Jordan was sleeping in his bunk about a quarter of a

The remains of U.S. Marines killed in Lebanon lie in state at Dover Air Force Base.

mile away when the attack occurred. The blast ripped the door off his hut. Major Jordan quickly rushed to what was left of the Aviation Safety Building. "I have not seen carnage like this since Vietnam," he said. "Marines were staggering out of the ruins trying to help each other. We heard voices from the rubble and tried to get to the wounded."

10   Surviving Marines tried desperately to find their missing buddies. One survivor was a soldier who had been standing guard at the time of the attack. "It was unbelievable. I saw the truck crash though the entrance, and then the explosion threw me against the wall," he said. "My God, I must be the last person left alive in my section. I don't know why I'm living."

11   Sometimes in disasters like this, there are small miracles. Mostly, the rescue workers found dead Marines. But as one search team was digging through the ruins, a head suddenly was uncovered. Slowly, the rescuers dug out the man's arms and legs. Although badly wounded, this Marine was alive.

12   Incredibly, the terrorists did not seem satisfied with the morning's bloodshed. For two hours in the afternoon, snipers in nearby buildings fired shots at the rescue workers. Luckily, they did not kill anyone. Still, the flying bullets were a reminder of how vulnerable the survivors were.

13   President Ronald Reagan expressed the anger and shock felt by most Americans.

"I know there are no words to properly express our outrage and the outrage of all Americans at this despicable act," said Reagan. He went on to say that the United States would not be driven out of Lebanon. Terrorists, he said, "cannot take that vital and strategic area of the earth."

14   Despite these brave words, the United States pulled out of Lebanon a few months later. If the goal of the terrorists had been to drive the United States out of Lebanon, they succeeded. The Marines had been given an impossible mission. They could not solve the religious and ethnic issues that have divided the people of Lebanon for centuries. The tragedy was that it took the lives of those 241 young men to reach this conclusion. 🍃

If you have been timed while reading this article, enter your reading time below. Then turn to the Words-per-Minute Table on page 195 and look up your reading speed (words per minute). Enter your reading speed on the graph on page 196.

Reading Time: Lesson 18

_____ : _____
Minutes   Seconds

A Finding the Main Idea

One statement below expresses the main idea of the article. One statement is too general, or too broad. The other statement explains only part of the article; it is too narrow. Label the statements using the following key:

M—Main Idea   **B—Too Broad**   **N—Too Narrow**

_____ 1. Lebanon had been plagued by political, religious, and ethnic conflicts for years.

_____ 2. The truck that slammed into the Marine barracks was filled with 5,000 pounds of explosives.

_____ 3. In 1983, a terrorist group attacked a Marine barracks in Beirut, killing 241 men.

_____ Score 15 points for a correct M answer.

_____ Score 5 points for each correct B or N answer.

_____ **Total Score:** Finding the Main Idea

B Recalling Facts

How well do you remember the facts in the article? Put an X in the box next to the answer that correctly completes each statement about the article.

1. The peacekeeping Marines lived

☐ a. in secure bunkers.

☐ b. in the lawless streets of Beirut.

☐ c. at the edge of the Beirut airport.

2. While patrolling the streets, six Marines were killed by

☐ a. snipers.

☐ b. French paratroopers.

☐ c. the government of Iran.

3. The terrorists attacked on a Sunday because they knew that

☐ a. most of the Marines would be asleep.

☐ b. some of the Marines would be at church.

☐ c. no one would be in the building.

4. The man rescue workers found while digging through the ruins was

☐ a. one of the terrorists.

☐ b. Major Robert Jordan.

☐ c. badly wounded but still alive.

5. A few months after the terrorist attack in Beirut,

☐ a. President Reagan expressed his outrage over the attack.

☐ b. the United States pulled out of Lebanon.

☐ c. the United States vowed to stay in Lebanon.

_____ Score 5 points for each correct answer.

_____ **Total Score:** Recalling Facts

C | Making Inferences

When you combine your own experience and information from a text to draw a conclusion that is not directly stated in that text, you are making an inference. Below are five statements that may or may not be inferences based on information in the article. Label the statements using the following key:

C—Correct Inference   F—Faulty Inference

_____ 1. The driver of the Mercedes truck was not killed in the bombing of the Marine barracks.

_____ 2. The American government did nothing at all to protect the lives of the peacekeeping Marines in Beirut.

_____ 3. The attack had no effect on American policy in Lebanon.

_____ 4. Many people in Lebanon did not welcome U.S. involvement in the country's affairs.

_____ 5. Immediately after the bombing, all the terrorists in the area fled the scene.

Score 5 points for each correct answer.

_____ **Total Score:** Making Inferences

D | Using Words Precisely

Each numbered sentence below contains an underlined word or phrase from the article. Following the sentence are three definitions. One definition is closest to the meaning of the underlined word. One definition is opposite or nearly opposite. Label those two definitions using the following key. Do not label the remaining definition.

C—Closest   O—Opposite or Nearly Opposite

1. That put them in a <u>vulnerable</u> location.

    _____ a. remote

    _____ b. protected

    _____ c. defenseless

2. Lebanon had been racked by religious and ethnic <u>strife</u> for years.

    _____ a. conflict

    _____ b. laws

    _____ c. peace

3. Defense Minister Charles Hernu called the bombing "an <u>odious</u> and cowardly attack."

    _____ a. delightful

    _____ b. hateful

    _____ c. unusual

4. "I know there are no words to properly express our outrage and the outrage of all Americans at this <u>despicable</u> act," said Reagan.

    _____ a. shameful

    _____ b. honorable

    _____ c. complicated

5. Terrorists, he said, "cannot take that <u>vital</u> and strategic area of the earth."

_____ a. uninhabited

_____ b. unnecessary

_____ c. critical

_____ Score 3 points for each correct C answer.

_____ Score 2 points for each correct O answer.

_____ **Total Score:** Using Words Precisely

Enter the four total scores in the spaces below, and add them together to find your Reading Comprehension Score. Then record your score on the graph on page 197.

Score	Question Type	Lesson 18
_____	Finding the Main Idea	
_____	Recalling Facts	
_____	Making Inferences	
_____	Using Words Precisely	
_____	**Reading Comprehension Score**	

Author's Approach

Put an X in the box next to the correct answer.

1. From the statements below, choose those that you believe the author would agree with.

☐ a. The Marines in Beirut should have been better protected.

☐ b. The Marines' peacekeeping mission helped improve conditions in Beirut.

☐ c. The terrorists wanted to drive the American military out of Lebanon.

2. In this article, "The Marines were, in short, sitting ducks if an enemy wanted to strike" means that the Marines

☐ a. shared the airport with a lot of wildlife.

☐ b. would be defenseless against an enemy attack.

☐ c. would only sit back and watch if the enemy chose to attack.

3. Choose the statement below that best describes the author's position in paragraph 14.

☐ a. The Marines failed in their mission to solve the religious and ethnic divisions in Lebanon.

☐ b. The Marines should not have been sent on such an impossible mission.

☐ c. The terrorists in Lebanon were better fighters than the Marines.

4. The author probably wrote this article in order to

☐ a. tell the reader about a terrorist attack in Beirut.

☐ b. tell the reader about U.S. policy in the Middle East.

☐ c. compare the bombing in Beirut to the Vietnam War.

_____ Number of correct answers

Record your personal assessment of your work on the Critical Thinking Chart on page 198.

Summarizing and Paraphrasing

Follow the directions provided for questions 1 and 2. Put an X in the box next to the correct answer for question 3.

1. Complete the following one-sentence summary of the article using the lettered phrases from the phrase bank below. Write the letters on the lines.

> **Phrase Bank:**
> a. the terrorist attack on the Marine barracks
> b. a description of the conditions in Beirut in 1983
> c. the U.S. government's decision to pull out of Lebanon

The article about the Beirut bombing begins with _____, goes on to explain _____, and ends with _____.

2. Reread paragraph 6 in the article. Below, write a summary of the paragraph in no more than 25 words.

_____

_____

_____

Reread your summary and decide whether it covers the important ideas in the paragraph. Next, decide how to shorten the summary to 15 words or less without leaving out any essential information. Write this summary below.

_____

_____

3. Choose the best one-sentence paraphrase for the following sentence from the article:

"Authorities believe that the Hezbollah, a terrorist organization supported by the government of Iran, planned an attack that would kill as many Marines as possible."

☐ a. Terrorists in Iran wanted to kill as many Marines as they could.

☐ b. A terrorist group supported by the Iranian government probably planned the attack in order to kill Marines.

☐ c. Authorities in the Iranian government believed that the terrorist organization wanted to kill as many Marines as possible.

> _____ Number of correct answers
>
> Record your personal assessment of your work on the Critical Thinking Chart on page 198.

Critical Thinking

Put an X in the box next to the correct answer for questions 1 and 3. Follow the directions provided for the other questions.

1. From what Major Jordan said, you can predict that

☐ a. the scene at the Marine barracks looked like a war zone.

☐ b. he has never fought in a war.

☐ c. he was too stunned to help injured Marines.

2. Choose from the letters below to correctly complete the following statement. Write the letters on the lines.

In the article, _____ and _____ are alike.

   a. the reaction of Defense Minister Charles Hernu to the bombing of the French barracks

   b. the reaction of President Ronald Reagan to the bombing of the Marine barracks

   c. the reaction of members of the Hezbollah to both bombings

3. What was the effect of ramming a truck loaded with explosives into a barracks filled with French soldiers?

   ☐ a. More people were killed at the American barracks.

   ☐ b. The blast moved the building 30 feet.

   ☐ c. The United States pulled out of Lebanon.

4. In which paragraph did you find the information or details to answer question 3?

_____ Number of correct answers

Record your personal assessment of your work on the Critical Thinking Chart on page 198.

Personal Response

I agree with the author because

Self-Assessment

Before reading this article, I already knew

CRITICAL THINKING

ATOMIC MELTDOWN AT CHERNOBYL

At a nuclear power plant in Sweden one Monday morning, a worker walked past a radiation detector and set off the dreaded alarm. Officials quickly checked his clothing and were shocked to find dangerously high levels of radiation. Fearing a deadly radiation leak, officials evacuated the plant. They tested all 600 employees to determine if they, too, were "hot"—and they were! Officials then tested the ground and found five times the normal level of radiation. But inside the plant, there was nothing wrong. What was going on?

2 The Swedes alerted the United States when other power stations around the country also reported high radiation levels. Soon reports of radiation poured in from Finland, Norway, and Denmark. Although the Swedes were relieved that the source of radiation was not their own country, they wanted to know where it was coming from. Had there been a nuclear explosion somewhere?

3 By Monday afternoon, April 28, 1986, Swedish officials had figured out that the atomic fallout was being carried by the wind. Scientists studied the radioactive

A protective wall (at left in photo) was constructed around the damaged area of the nuclear reactor at Chernobyl.

material and the wind pattern and concluded that a nuclear accident had indeed occurred. They tracked the radioactive cloud to Ukraine, a republic in the former Soviet Union.

4   A Swedish diplomat in Moscow, meanwhile, began to ask probing questions. But for 12 hours there was no reply from the Soviet government. Even the Soviet people were kept in the dark. Finally, at 9 P.M., the Soviets announced that there had been a nuclear reactor accident at the Chernobyl power plant. No casualties or other details on the worst nuclear accident in history were reported that night. The Soviets also kept secret that the explosion had happened three full days before.

5   From satellite photographs, scientists in the United States viewed the Chernobyl disaster. An explosion had blown the roof off a huge atomic reactor. Walls around the reactor bulged out, and in the center of the wreckage, a white hot fire was blazing.

6   Chernobyl is located 80 miles north of Kiev, the capital of Ukraine. The nuclear facility was old and poorly built. Inside its reactors were graphite bricks that could stop or slow down the nuclear chain reaction. Graphite, a form of carbon, was used to absorb radiation. But graphite is dangerous. If it catches fire, it can reach temperatures of more than 5,000 degrees Celsius. Because of this, most modern nuclear power plants no longer use graphite reactors. And they reinforce the buildings that house their atomic reactors with a concrete shell. The shell is designed to prevent radioactive materials from escaping during an accident. Chernobyl did not have this safety device. So when one of its reactors exploded and the graphite ignited, radioactive debris escaped freely into the air.

7   The Soviets moved quickly but quietly shortly after the accident. They sealed off the power plant and started to evacuate residents who lived within 19 miles of the facility. Some 50,000 people had to leave all their belongings behind and board buses and trains that would take them

The massive amounts of radiation released in the Chernobyl accident resulted in deformities in children born in the years immediately following the accident.

away from Chernobyl. Medical teams, scientists, and other experts arrived at the scene. Doctors were shocked to find people whose skin had turned brown. Their hair and eyelashes had fallen out. They felt weak and sick. One man said when he got out of his bed and stood up, the skin on his leg slipped off as if it had been a stocking. Some victims were so "hot" that even the doctors treating them became dangerously exposed.

8   The situation at Chernobyl worsened each day, yet the Soviets said little and asked for little from the outside world. They desperately tried to put out the raging graphite fire at the plant. Huge helicopters were brought in to attack the fire from the air. To protect the pilots from radiation, sheets of lead were placed under their seats. The brave pilots repeatedly flew over the reactor and dropped clay, lead, sand, and other materials on the inferno. They did not use water because it would have only fueled the flames. It took more than 5,000 tons of materials and 12 days to put out the fire. When ground crews could get near the plant, they bored tunnels under the concrete slab that supported the reactor. Water was then pumped into the tunnels to lower the temperature of the burning reactor core.

9   The area around Chernobyl remained "hot" for months after the accident. Work

crews had to limit the time they spent near the reactor, so the cleanup took longer. There was so much contaminated soil that the government didn't know where to bury it all. As for the damaged reactor, officials decided to encase it in a gigantic coffin. Trucks carrying ready-mix cement poured it into specially made steel vats. The cement-filled vats were like bricks. They formed a concrete wall, the "coffin," around the reactor.

10   The cleanup and safety measures taken by the Soviets did little to satisfy the rest of the world. The radioactive fallout had covered large sections of Ukraine and other parts of the former Soviet Union before spreading across most of Europe. Europeans were outraged. They accepted that the nuclear blast had been an accident, but they were furious that the Soviets tried to hide what happened. They were denied the chance to protect themselves.

11   Radioactive fallout contaminated water, land, livestock, and food supplies. Poland, which had radiation levels as high as 100,000 times the normal level, feared for the lives of its children. People were told not to eat farm products or drink milk from cows. In Norway, Sweden, and Finland, people were told not to drink or use rain water or eat freshwater fish. Officials in Italy banned the sales of some

food because they were "hot." In Scotland farmers could not sell the meat from their sheep because the animals had grazed on contaminated grass.

12   The Soviets claimed that only 31 people died because of Chernobyl, but the actual number is much higher. Since the accident, countless new cases of cancer have developed. Scientists estimate that perhaps more victims may die from the Chernobyl blast than all the people killed in World War II. And many areas affected by Chernobyl will remain "hot" for thousands of years, too "hot" to sustain life.

If you have been timed while reading this article, enter your reading time below. Then turn to the Words-per-Minute Table on page 195 and look up your reading speed (words per minute). Enter your reading speed on the graph on page 196.

Reading Time: Lesson 19

_____ : _____

Minutes   Seconds

A | Finding the Main Idea

One statement below expresses the main idea of the article. One statement is too general, or too broad. The other statement explains only part of the article; it is too narrow. Label the statements using the following key:

M—Main Idea   **B—Too Broad**   **N—Too Narrow**

_____ 1. A nuclear explosion resulted in widespread contamination.

_____ 2. In 1986, the Soviet Union experienced a serious nuclear accident resulting in sickness and death and then tried to hide it from the world.

_____ 3. The Soviet Union claimed that 31 people died as a direct result of the Chernobyl accident.

_____ Score 15 points for a correct M answer.

_____ Score 5 points for each correct B or N answer.

_____ **Total Score:** Finding the Main Idea

B | Recalling Facts

How well do you remember the facts in the article? Put an X in the box next to the answer that correctly completes each statement about the article.

1. High radiation levels were first noticed by
   ☐ a. Russia.
   ☐ b. Sweden.
   ☐ c. a United States satellite.

2. Chernobyl is located north of
   ☐ a. Ukraine.
   ☐ b. Kiev.
   ☐ c. Moscow.

3. Most modern nuclear reactors
   ☐ a. have had at least one major accident.
   ☐ b. are surrounded by a protective shell.
   ☐ c. operate without any risks.

4. Many European countries
   ☐ a. were seriously affected by the radiation.
   ☐ b. sympathized with the Soviets.
   ☐ c. were not at all harmed by the accident.

5. In an attempt to contain the radiation, Soviet officials decided to
   ☐ a. flood the reactor.
   ☐ b. move the reactor to an uninhabited area.
   ☐ c. enclose the reactor in a concrete coffin.

Score 5 points for each correct answer.

_____ **Total Score:** Recalling Facts

C Making Inferences

When you combine your own experience and information from a text to draw a conclusion that is not directly stated in that text, you are making an inference. Below are five statements that may or may not be inferences based on information in the article. Label the statements using the following key:

C—Correct Inference   **F—Faulty Inference**

_____ 1. At the time of the accident, not much was known about nuclear power.

_____ 2. Soviet nuclear reactors are safer than American reactors.

_____ 3. Swedish officials feared a serious radiation leak at one of their nuclear plants.

_____ 4. Norway and Finland reported the highest levels of radioactive fallout.

_____ 5. The Soviets were capable of handling the disaster by themselves.

Score 5 points for each correct answer.

_____ **Total Score:** Making Inferences

D Using Words Precisely

Each numbered sentence below contains an underlined word or phrase from the article. Following the sentence are three definitions. One definition is closest to the meaning of the underlined word. One definition is opposite or nearly opposite. Label those two definitions using the following key. Do not label the remaining definition.

C—Closest   **O—Opposite or Nearly Opposite**

1. The Swedes <u>alerted</u> the United States when other power stations around the country also reported high radiation levels.

_____ a. blamed

_____ b. informed

_____ c. kept a secret from

2. A Swedish diplomat in Moscow, meanwhile, began to ask <u>probing</u> questions.

_____ a. pointless

_____ b. many

_____ c. searching

3. There was so much <u>contaminated</u> soil that the government didn't know where to bury it all.

_____ a. healthy and pure

_____ b. tainted and poisoned

_____ c. rocky

4. Europeans were <u>outraged</u>.

_____ a. furious

_____ b. pleased

_____ c. amused

5. And many areas affected by Chernobyl will remain...too "hot" to <u>sustain</u> life.

_____ a. support and maintain

_____ b. destroy

_____ c. discover

_____ Score 3 points for each correct C answer.

_____ Score 2 points for each correct O answer.

_____ **Total Score:** Using Words Precisely

Enter the four total scores in the spaces below, and add them together to find your Reading Comprehension Score. Then record your score on the graph on page 197.

Score	Question Type	Lesson 19
_____	Finding the Main Idea	
_____	Recalling Facts	
_____	Making Inferences	
_____	Using Words Precisely	
_____	**Reading Comprehension Score**	

Author's Approach

Put an X in the box next to the correct answer.

1. The author uses the first sentence of the article to
   - [ ] a. explain how radiation from Chernobyl was detected in Sweden.
   - [ ] b. describe a nuclear power plant in Sweden.
   - [ ] c. describe safety procedures at a power plant in Sweden.

2. In this article, "And many areas affected by Chernobyl will remain 'hot' for thousands of years, too 'hot' to sustain life" means
   - [ ] a. the radiation levels in these areas will be too high to support life.
   - [ ] b. the temperature in these areas will be too high to support life.
   - [ ] c. people won't be able to live in these areas for political reasons.

3. The author probably wrote this article in order to
   - [ ] a. convince the reader that the Soviet Union acted irresponsibly.
   - [ ] b. compare technology in the former Soviet Union with that in other parts of the world.
   - [ ] c. inform the reader about the worst nuclear accident in history.

4. How is the author's purpose for writing the article expressed in paragraph 8?
   - [ ] a. The author tries to persuade the reader that the Soviet Union did everything it could to cover up the accident.
   - [ ] b. The author tells the reader what the Soviets did to try to put out the graphite fire at the plant.
   - [ ] c. The author points out that a graphite fire would not have occurred in modern plants in other parts of the world.

_____ Number of correct answers

Record your personal assessment of your work on the Critical Thinking Chart on page 198.

CRITICAL THINKING

Summarizing and Paraphrasing

Follow the directions provided for questions 1 and 2. Put an X in the box next to the correct answer for question 3.

1. Look for the important ideas and events in paragraphs 2 and 3. Summarize those paragraphs in one or two sentences.

_____

_____

_____

2. Reread paragraph 7 in the article. Below, write a summary of the paragraph in no more than 25 words.

_____

_____

_____

_____

Reread your summary and decide whether it covers the important ideas in the paragraph. Next, decide how to shorten the summary to 15 words or less without leaving out any essential information. Write this summary below.

_____

_____

_____

3. Read the statement about the article below. Then read the paraphrase of that statement. Choose the reason that best tells why the paraphrase does not say the same thing as the statement.

Statement: Although Europeans realized that the nuclear disaster in Chernobyl was an accident, they were angry because the Soviets' secrecy denied Europeans the chance to protect themselves from the fallout.

Paraphrase: Europeans were unable to protect themselves from the fallout resulting from the nuclear accident in Chernobyl.

☐ a. Paraphrase says too much.

☐ b. Paraphrase doesn't say enough.

☐ c. Paraphrase doesn't agree with the statement about the article.

_____ Number of correct answers

Record your personal assessment of your work on the Critical Thinking Chart on page 198.

Critical Thinking

Put an X in the box next to the correct answer for questions 1, 3, and 4. Follow the directions provided for question 2.

1. From the events in the article, you can predict that the following will happen next:

☐ a. People will return to Chernobyl once the danger has passed.

☐ b. All of the nuclear reactors in the world will be closed down to prevent another terrible accident.

☐ c. The safety measures in nuclear reactors around the world will become stricter.

CRITICAL THINKING

2. Choose from the letters below to correctly complete the following statement. Write the letters on the lines.

In the article, _____ and _____ were alike.

a. the level of alarm about public safety in the United States

b. the level of alarm about public safety in Norway

c. the level of alarm about public safety in Finland

3. What was the cause of the high radiation levels reported in Sweden?

☐ a. There had been an explosion at a nuclear reactor at the Chernobyl power plant.

☐ b. There had been an explosion at a nuclear reactor in a Swedish power plant.

☐ c. For three full days, the Soviets kept the explosion a secret.

4. How is the meltdown at Chernobyl an example of a disaster?

☐ a. The power plant was shown to be poorly made.

☐ b. Relations between Europe and the Soviet Union suffered as a result of the accident.

☐ c. The accident killed many people and put the lives of thousands of others in danger.

_____ Number of correct answers

Record your personal assessment of your work on the Critical Thinking Chart on page 198.

Personal Response

If you could ask the author of the article one question, what would it be?

_____

_____

_____

_____

Self-Assessment

The part I found most difficult about the article was

_____

_____

_____

I found this difficult because

_____

_____

_____

_____

CRITICAL THINKING

THE SAN FRANCISCO EARTHQUAKE

After the earthquake, fires erupted throughout San Francisco. Here, San Franciscans watch their city burn from the top of Russian Hill.

On April 18, 1906, at 5:12 A.M., San Francisco was rocked by a great earthquake. Although the quake itself lasted just seconds, it was indirectly responsible for the destruction of three-fourths of the entire city. About 300,000 people were made homeless, and 38,000 buildings were destroyed.

2 The earthquake itself caused little of this damage. The principal destructive force was the fire caused by the quake. Survivors of the San Francisco disaster have always referred to it, not as "the Earthquake of 1906" but as "the great Fire of 1906."

3 San Francisco was a very modern city in 1906, and its modern power system was responsible for its destruction. The shock of the quake broke petroleum tanks, and the upheaval of the streets snapped gas mains. All the situation needed to set off a giant conflagration was one spark, and there were sparks aplenty from the broken overhead electric wires. Within seconds, a large part of the city was on fire.

4 Unfortunately, one of the victims of the quake was the head of the city's fire

department. He was crushed to death when the chimney of his home fell on top of him.

5 The fire department was handicapped not only by the tragic loss of its leader but also by the loss of almost all of its water supply. The tremor had snapped the water mains buried deep in the ground. Moreover, the quake had destroyed the city's fire alarm boxes and all telephone communications.

6 Even if the firefighters could have received orders, it would have been difficult for them to report to their firehouses since travel, including public transportation, had been brought to a standstill. Train and streetcar lines suffered twisted rails from the upheaval of the streets. During the first few hours after the quake, individual firefighters and small fire companies could do little more than help extricate victims who were lying helpless, pinned under the wreckage of collapsed buildings.

7 All civil authorities were as handicapped as the fire department. However, a large military post was located in San Francisco. General Frederick Funston, United States Army, commanded the troops in San Francisco. As a young man, Funston had tried to get into West Point but had failed the Military Academy's entrance exam. He enlisted in the army as a private, and his heroism brought him rapid promotion. During service in the Philippine Islands, he won the Congressional Medal of Honor, the highest award the United States gives for valor.

8 Now, with the city in flames, and the police and fire departments overwhelmed, General Funston took charge. He placed the city under martial law and ordered his troops into the streets. The soldiers carried loaded rifles with bayonets and had orders to "shoot to kill" to prevent looting. Many people had been forced to flee from their homes with only the clothes on their backs. These refugees, in their haste and confusion, had abandoned their homes and valuables, often without even remaining behind long enough to lock their doors. The troops were assigned to protect homes from roving bands of robbers.

9 AThe troops' second assignment was to use dynamite and artillery to blow up buildings in the line of the fire's advance. This would create firebreaks, flat areas in the path of the fire that would halt its advance by denying it any fuel on which it could feed. Some of the firebreaks did work to slow down the spread of the conflagration. Often, however, before the troops could detonate the dynamite they had planted, the rapidly advancing blaze set it off. The premature explosions hurled flaming wreckage onto buildings not yet touched by the flames. Thus, the dynamiting, rather than retarding the advance of the blaze, sometimes spread it to new areas.

10 The troops' other mission, the prevention of looting, accomplished a

Houses on Howard Street in San Francisco are set askew as a result of the earthquake.

great deal of good, but it also did some harm. The presence of armed soldiers did discourage some would-be looters, but the troops also shot or bayoneted some innocent citizens who were trying to remove their own valuables from their homes before the flames reached them. There is also some evidence that a few soldiers actually became looters themselves, stealing the very property that they were supposed to be guarding.

11   One section of the city that did not fall victim to either the fire or the dynamiters was the area known as Telegraph Hill. The Italian families who lived there fought the fire block by block and house by house. They fought with brooms and blankets and buckets of water from San Francisco Bay. And when there was no water, they fought with barrels of homemade red wine from their cellars. They fought— and they won.

12   Three days after the earthquake, the flames began to come under control. As the blaze approached the waterfront, the city's firefighters, aided by forces from nearby cities, were able to draw water from San Francisco Bay. Their efforts, combined with a shift in wind direction, finally brought the flames under control.

13   Three-fourths of the city had been destroyed by the quake and the fires that followed. About 700 people had lost their lives, and many of the people who survived felt that they had been touched by God—and spared.

14   Within five years after the earthquake, San Francisco had been rebuilt and showed no signs of the destruction left by the quake or the fire. Today, San Francisco is one of the largest cities in the United States. And its residents know all about the danger of earthquakes. In 1989 the strongest quake since 1906 hit the Bay Area, killing 55 people and causing billions of dollars worth of damage.

If you have been timed while reading this article, enter your reading time below. Then turn to the Words-per-Minute Table on page 195 and look up your reading speed (words per minute). Enter your reading speed on the graph on page 196.

Reading Time: **Lesson 20**

_____ : _____
Minutes   Seconds

A | Finding the Main Idea

One statement below expresses the main idea of the article. One statement is too general, or too broad. The other statement explains only part of the article; it is too narrow. Label the statements using the following key:

M—Main Idea   **B—Too Broad**   **N—Too Narrow**

_____ 1. Earthquakes and fires can be a deadly combination.

_____ 2. Broken power and gas lines set off fires throughout San Francisco.

_____ 3. The San Francisco earthquake and the fires it caused were responsible for death and destruction in 1906.

_____ Score 15 points for a correct M answer.

_____ Score 5 points for each correct B or N answer.

_____ **Total Score:** Finding the Main Idea

B | Recalling Facts

How well do you remember the facts in the article? Put an X in the box next to the answer that correctly completes each statement about the article.

1. After the quake, streetcars were not running because the
    - ☐ a. motormen who were supposed to drive them did not show up for work.
    - ☐ b. tracks were twisted.
    - ☐ c. the general ordered them shut down.

2. The fire department was hampered by
    - ☐ a. interference from the soldiers.
    - ☐ b. lack of water.
    - ☐ c. homeowners who feared the firefighters would loot their homes.

3. Dynamiting buildings
    - ☐ a. sometimes resulted in spreading the fire.
    - ☐ b. was entirely successful in stopping the fire.
    - ☐ c. prevented looting.

4. The quake and the resulting fires left
    - ☐ a. 3,000 people homeless.
    - ☐ b. 38,000 people homeless.
    - ☐ c. 300,000 people homeless.

5. When the Italian families on Telegraph Hill ran out of water, they
    - ☐ a. stopped fighting the fire and fled for their lives.
    - ☐ b. threw homemade wine on the fire.
    - ☐ c. got more water from San Francisco Bay.

Score 5 points for each correct answer.

_____ **Total Score:** Recalling Facts

C Making Inferences

When you combine your own experience and information from a text to draw a conclusion that is not directly stated in that text, you are making an inference. Below are five statements that may or may not be inferences based on information in the article. Label the statements using the following key:

C—Correct Inference   F—Faulty Inference

_____ 1. It was fortunate that a large military post was located in San Francisco.

_____ 2. General Funston was a brave man.

_____ 3. The troops called in to prevent looting did more harm than good.

_____ 4. The residents of Telegraph Hill showed a tremendous amount of determination.

_____ 5. Although many years have passed since the earthquake of 1906, San Francisco has never fully recovered.

Score 5 points for each correct answer.

_____ **Total Score:** Making Inferences

D Using Words Precisely

Each numbered sentence below contains an underlined word or phrase from the article. Following the sentence are three definitions. One definition is closest to the meaning of the underlined word. One definition is opposite or nearly opposite. Label those two definitions using the following key. Do not label the remaining definition.

C—Closest   O—Opposite or Nearly Opposite

1. The shock of the quake broke petroleum tanks, and the <u>upheaval</u> of the streets snapped gas mains.

_____ a. confusion

_____ b. sinking

_____ c. lifting from below

2. …firefighters and small fire companies could do little more than help <u>extricate</u> victims who were lying helpless, pinned under the wreckage of collapsed buildings

_____ a. push back

_____ b. pull out

_____ c. identify

3. During service in the Philippine Islands, he [General Funston] won the…highest award the United States gave for <u>valor</u>.

_____ a. bravery

_____ b. creativity

_____ c. cowardice

4. He placed the city under <u>martial</u> law and ordered his troops into the streets.

_____ a. state

_____ b. military

_____ c. civilian

5. Thus, the dynamiting, rather than <u>retarding</u> the advance of the blaze, sometimes spread it to new areas.

_____ a. slowing down

_____ b. speeding up

_____ c. alerting others about

_____ Score 3 points for each correct C answer.

_____ Score 2 points for each correct O answer.

_____ **Total Score:** Using Words Precisely

Enter the four total scores in the spaces below, and add them together to find your Reading Comprehension Score. Then record your score on the graph on page 197.

Score	Question Type	Lesson 20
_____	Finding the Main Idea	
_____	Recalling Facts	
_____	Making Inferences	
_____	Using Words Precisely	
_____	**Reading Comprehension Score**	

Author's Approach

Put an X in the box next to the correct answer.

1. The main purpose of the first paragraph is to

☐ a. compare the earthquake's damage to that caused by the fire.

☐ b. describe San Francisco in the early 1900s.

☐ c. describe the devastation caused by the 1906 earthquake in San Francisco.

2. Which of the following statements from the article best describes General Funston's military record?

☐ a. "As a young man Funston had tried to get into West Point but had failed the Military Academy's entrance exam."

☐ b. "General Frederick Funston, United States Army, commanded the troops in San Francisco."

☐ c. "During service in the Philippine Islands, he won the Congressional Medal of Honor, the highest award the United States gives for valor."

3. From the statements below, choose those that you believe the author would agree with.

☐ a. Funston's troops helped protect people's homes and possessions.

☐ b. The city's fire department could have done a lot more to fight the fires.

☐ c. The people of San Francisco worked hard to rebuild their city.

CRITICAL THINKING

4. The author tells this story mainly by

☐ a. comparing the earthquake in 1906 to the one in 1989.

☐ b. telling how the people of San Francisco responded to the quake and fire.

☐ c. retelling the personal experiences of the Italian families on Telegraph Hill.

_____ Number of correct answers

Record your personal assessment of your work on the Critical Thinking Chart on page 198.

Summarizing and Paraphrasing

Follow the directions provided for question 1. Put an X in the box next to the correct answer for question 2.

1. Complete the following one-sentence summary of the article using the lettered phrases from the phrase bank below. Write the letters on the lines.

Phrase Bank:
a. the fire's end and the effects of the disaster
b. General Funston's efforts to take charge of the situation
c. the destructive force of the earthquake and fire

The article about the 1906 San Francisco earthquake begins with _____, goes on to explain _____, and ends with _____.

2. Choose the sentence that correctly restates the following sentence from the article:

"Even if the firefighters could have received orders, it would have been difficult for them to report to their firehouses since travel, including public transportation, had been brought to a standstill."

☐ a. The firefighters had received orders to close down public transportation and report to their firehouses.

☐ b. Firefighters did not receive their orders because public transportation had been halted.

☐ c. Firefighters did not receive orders, but even if they had, they could not have reached their firehouses because public transportation had been halted.

_____ Number of correct answers

Record your personal assessment of your work on the Critical Thinking Chart on page 198.

Critical Thinking

Follow the directions provided for questions 1, 3, 4, and 5. Put an X in the box next to the correct answer for question 2.

1. For each statement below, write O if it expresses an opinion and write F if it expresses a fact.

_____ a. The 1989 earthquake in the Bay Area killed 55 people and caused billions of dollars worth of damage.

_____ b. The head of the city's fire department was crushed to death by his own chimney.

_____ c. People spared by the quake and fire had been touched by God.

2. From the information in paragraph 11, you can predict that

☐ a. in the future, the fire department used wine to combat fires.

☐ b. looters didn't bother the Italian families on Telegraph Hill.

☐ c. in the future, the fire department used brooms and blankets to combat fires.

3. Choose from the letters below to correctly complete the following statement. Write the letters on the lines.

On the positive side, _____, but on the negative side _____.

a. General Funston failed to get into West Point

b. many people were killed and many others were left homeless by the disaster

c. San Francisco was completely rebuilt five years after the quake and fire

4. Think about cause-effect relationships in the article. Fill in the blanks in the cause-effect chart, drawing from the letters below.

Cause   Effect

The tremor snapped the city's water mains.   _____

_____   The dynamiting spread the fire.

_____   Looters robbed many homes.

a. Some people, fleeing the fires, forgot to lock their doors.

b. The fire sometimes caused the dynamite to explode too soon.

c. The fire department lost most of its water supply.

5. Which paragraphs from the article provide evidence that supports your answer to question 4?

_____

_____ Number of correct answers

Record your personal assessment of your work on the Critical Thinking Chart on page 198.

Personal Response

Why do you think General Funston took charge of the situation in San Francisco?

_____

_____

_____

_____

Self-Assessment

While reading the article, I found it easiest to

_____

_____

_____

BOSTON'S GREAT MOLASSES FLOOD

Have you ever heard someone described as being "slower than molasses in January"? Molasses is a thick, sticky, sugary syrup that moves very slowly when it is poured. And the colder it is, the stickier and slower-moving molasses becomes. But one January afternoon—January 15, 1919—molasses moved so fast that it snuffed out the lives of 21 people and destroyed a large section of Boston's North End.

2   For nearly three centuries, molasses played a key role in Boston's economy. Colonists used molasses in place of high-priced sugar. They also used the sticky syrup to make and sell their own rum. The community of Boston depended on the trade generated from the sale and manufacture of molasses.

3   Ironically, the molasses industry was about to suffer a devastating blow that fateful January. Only one more state's vote was needed to approve Prohibition, the 18th Amendment to the United States Constitution, and the vote was certain. With Nebraska's approval, the sale and manufacture of any alcoholic beverage would become illegal. The passage of Prohibition would spell disaster for the

This section of elevated train structure in Boston is a twisted mass of metal as a result of the "Great Molasses Flood of 1919."

molasses industry. But before the dreaded news from Nebraska could spread across the North End community, Boston's massive molasses tank exploded.

4   The huge metal tank loomed high above Commercial Street, near Boston's harbor, supported by a frame of metal legs. The tank itself was 50 feet tall; and it was almost 300 feet (the length of a football field) around. Inside the tank were steam pipes that kept the molasses warm.

On January 12, the tank was filled beyond its capacity. It was intended to hold almost 2 million gallons of molasses, but on that day the tank held more than 2.3 million gallons.

5   January 15 was an unusually warm day in Boston. At midday people were outdoors enjoying the sunshine. Workers from factories and warehouses were outside on loading docks eating lunch. And many of the North End shopkeepers and residents,

This building and the surrounding area show the extent of the damage caused by the molasses flood.

newly arrived immigrants from Italy, were standing in doorways. They remarked how the warm weather was reminiscent of their sunny home country.

6 Suddenly, the balmy day was shattered by a deep rumbling sound…then a series of deafening explosions. The molasses tank had burst open! A flood of steaming hot liquid gushed out and poured down Commercial Street. And there was nothing slow about the way this molasses ran that January afternoon. People in its path couldn't run fast enough to avoid it. The sludge grabbed their feet and swirled them around. Other people scrambled to keep ahead of the sticky, 30-foot-high wave of molasses, but it was hopeless. Twenty-seven million pounds of the sticky goo poured over walkers, lunch crowds, and factory workers. It demolished buildings and lifted some right off their foundations. Twenty-one people were ether crushed by the wreckage or drowned in the gooey substance in a matter of minutes.

7 Meanwhile, a northbound train on Boston's new elevated railway was heading straight for disaster. As the train rounded a curve, the brakeman suddenly saw the raging flood of molasses before him. He quickly pulled the emergency cord, and the train stopped, just barely avoiding a deadly plunge into the swirling sea of molasses below. Flying pieces of the broken tank had sliced through the 15-inch supporting shafts of the elevated tracks, toppling them into the savage flood.

8 Although there were cars and trucks back in the year 1919, most freight was still hauled by horses and wagons. Dozens of carts became trapped in the sticky sludge. Horses reared and snorted, rolling their eyes in terror as they found themselves mired in the ooze. Many of them were bowled over and suffocated. Those horses alive, but trapped in the syrup, were helpless and suffering. Police had to shoot some of the terrified beasts to put them out of their misery.

9 Many well-meaning bystanders who tried to help the trapped victims soon found themselves snared knee-deep in sticky molasses. The stuff was worse than quicksand. Rescuers had to cut people right out of their clothes in order to free them. The clothes had become crusted with crystallized sugar.

10 As weary rescuers and residents slowly returned to their homes, they spread the molasses all over the city. The next day every city bench in the area was sticky. Molasses covered buses, trees, roofs, and overhead wires. The cleanup went on for days. Even after the injured had been cared for and the dead had been buried, Boston continued to live a nightmare. It was weeks before the odor of molasses disappeared. And the waters of Boston Harbor had a brown cast for months afterward.

11 What caused the disaster? Purity Distilling Company, the firm that owned the tank, blamed the collapse on vibrations caused by a passing train. But most people didn't buy that explanation. Later, the company changed its story. It claimed that political anarchists had deliberately caused the explosion. Bostonians didn't buy that story either. Most people simply thought that the warm weather, coming in the midst of January's usual cold, had caused the molasses to heat up, expand, and burst the tank's seams.

12 There was, of course, an investigation. The official verdict was that the original workmanship of the tank had been shoddy. The tank's owners had to pay heavy damages to the families of victims and to those who lost property. But no amount of money could ever make up for the suffering and loss of 21 lives in what has become known as "Boston's Great Molasses Flood." 🍃

If you have been timed while reading this article, enter your reading time below. Then turn to the Words-per-Minute Table on page 195 and look up your reading speed (words per minute). Enter your reading speed on the graph on page 196.

Reading Time: **Lesson 21**

_____ : _____

Minutes   Seconds

A Finding the Main Idea

One statement below expresses the main idea of the article. One statement is too general, or too broad. The other statement explains only part of the article; it is too narrow. Label the statements using the following key:

M—Main Idea   **B—Too Broad**   **N—Too Narrow**

_____ 1. Many innocent people were killed in an accident in Boston's North End community.

_____ 2. Death and destruction occurred after a tank of molasses exploded onto a Boston street.

_____ 3. More than 2 million gallons of molasses raced through the streets of Boston one January day.

_____ Score 15 points for a correct M answer.

_____ Score 5 points for each correct B or N answer.

_____ **Total Score:** Finding the Main Idea

B Recalling Facts

How well do you remember the facts in the article? Put an X in the box next to the answer that correctly completes each statement about the article.

1. The day the tank burst was
   - ☐ a. unusually cold for January.
   - ☐ b. unusually warm for January.
   - ☐ c. very hot and humid.

2. When the tank burst there was
   - ☐ a. no sound.
   - ☐ b. a high, squealing sound.
   - ☐ c. a deep rumbling, then explosions.

3. The passage of Prohibition would have
   - ☐ a. improved Boston's molasses industry.
   - ☐ b. had no effect on Boston's molasses industry.
   - ☐ c. crippled Boston's molasses industry.

4. Well-meaning bystanders
   - ☐ a. became trapped in the gooey molasses.
   - ☐ b. rescued most of the victims.
   - ☐ c. were forced to leave the scene.

5. A northbound train
   - ☐ a. plunged into the molasses below.
   - ☐ b. was swept into the harbor.
   - ☐ c. nearly plunged into the sea of molasses.

Score 5 points for each correct answer.

_____ **Total Score:** Recalling Facts

C Making Inferences

When you combine your own experience and information from a text to draw a conclusion that is not directly stated in that text, you are making an inference. Below are five statements that may or may not be inferences based on information in the article. Label the statements using the following key:

C—Correct Inference   F—Faulty Inference

_____ 1. If the day had been colder more people would have died.

_____ 2. Police could have saved the trapped horses.

_____ 3. No one had the courage to help those stuck in the molasses.

_____ 4. The company that owned the tank was happy to accept responsibility for the accident.

_____ 5. The tank had been poorly constructed and was overfilled.

Score 5 points for each correct answer.

_____ **Total Score:** Making Inferences

D Using Words Precisely

Each numbered sentence below contains an underlined word or phrase from the article. Following the sentence are three definitions. One definition is closest to the meaning of the underlined word. One definition is opposite or nearly opposite. Label those two definitions using the following key. Do not label the remaining definition.

C—Closest   O—Opposite or Nearly Opposite

1. They remarked how the warm weather was reminiscent of their sunny home country.

_____ a. totally dissimilar to

_____ b. remindful of

_____ c. the misfortune of

2. Suddenly, the balmy day was shattered by a deep rumbling sound....

_____ a. early morning

_____ b. stormy and cold

_____ c. mild and pleasant

3. Horses reared and snorted, rolling their eyes in terror as they found themselves mired in the ooze.

_____ a. released from

_____ b. exhausted from

_____ c. trapped in

4. The clothes had become crusted with crystallized sugar.

_____ a. turned from liquid to solid

_____ b. melted

_____ c. spoiled

5. The official verdict was that the original workmanship of the tank had been <u>shoddy</u>.

_____ a. substandard

_____ b. famous

_____ c. superior

_____ Score 3 points for each correct C answer.

_____ Score 2 points for each correct O answer.

_____ **Total Score:** Using Words Precisely

Enter the four total scores in the spaces below, and add them together to find your Reading Comprehension Score. Then record your score on the graph on page 197.

Score	Question Type	Lesson 21
_____	Finding the Main Idea	
_____	Recalling Facts	
_____	Making Inferences	
_____	Using Words Precisely	
_____	**Reading Comprehension Score**	

Author's Approach

Put an X in the box next to the correct answer.

1. The main purpose of the first paragraph is to
   - ☐ a. inform the reader about someone who is very slow.
   - ☐ b. describe the qualities of molasses and to relate molasses to the disaster.
   - ☐ c. entertain the reader with a funny saying.

2. In this article, "As weary rescuers and residents slowly returned to their homes, they spread the molasses all over the city" means
   - ☐ a. the molasses stuck to people and they couldn't help but take the sticky stuff wherever they went.
   - ☐ b. people purposely spread the molasses all over the city.
   - ☐ c. the molasses had flowed all over the city.

3. Choose the statement below that best describes the author's position in paragraph 12.
   - ☐ a. The tank's owners had to pay too much money to compensate the families of the victims.
   - ☐ b. The tank's owners paid too little to compensate the families of the victims.
   - ☐ c. No amount of money could compensate the families of the victims.

4. The author probably wrote this article in order to
   - ☐ a. persuade the reader that the Purity Distilling Company was responsible for the molasses flood.
   - ☐ b. describe the characteristics of molasses.
   - ☐ c. inform the reader about the molasses flood in Boston.

_____ Number of correct answers

Record your personal assessment of your work on the Critical Thinking Chart on page 198.

Summarizing and Paraphrasing

Follow the directions provided for questions 1 and 2. Put an X in the box next to the correct answer for question 3.

1. Complete the following one-sentence summary of the article using the lettered phrases from the phrase bank below. Write the letters on the lines.

> **Phrase Bank:**
> a. what happened when the molasses tank burst
> b. a discussion of the molasses industry in Boston
> c. an investigation into what caused the disaster

After a short introduction, the article about Boston's molasses flood begins with _____, goes on to explain _____, and ends with _____.

2. Reread paragraph 8 in the article. Below, write a summary of the paragraph in no more than 25 words.

_____

_____

_____

Reread your summary and decide whether it covers the important ideas in the paragraph. Next, decide how to shorten the summary to 15 words or less without leaving out any essential information. Write this summary below.

_____

_____

3. Choose the best one-sentence paraphrase for the following sentence from the article:

"Most people simply thought that the warm weather, coming in the midst of January's usual cold, had caused the molasses to heat up, expand, and burst the tank's seams."

☐ a. Many people thought that the cold weather had caused the tank to burst.

☐ b. Many thought that the warm weather had caused the molasses to expand and split open the tank.

☐ c. Many people thought that the tank had expanded in the heat and burst its seams.

> _____ Number of correct answers
>
> Record your personal assessment of your work on the Critical Thinking Chart on page 198.

Critical Thinking

Put an X in the box next to the correct answer for question 1. Follow the directions provided for the other questions.

1. Judging from the brakeman's actions as told in this article, you can predict that

☐ a. there would have been many more casualties if he hadn't acted so quickly.

☐ b. he could have avoided disaster by driving the train through the flood.

☐ c. there would have been fewer casualties if he hadn't stopped the train.

CRITICAL THINKING

2. Using what you know about sudden, flash floods and what is told about Boston's molasses flood in the article, name three ways a flood of water is similar to and three ways it is different from a molasses flood. Cite the paragraph number(s) where you found details in the article to support your conclusions.

Similarities

_____

_____

_____

Differences

_____

_____

_____

3. Choose from the letters below to correctly complete the following statement. Write the letters on the lines.

According to the article, _____ caused _____, and the effect was _____.

a. them to get stuck in the molasses

b. rescuers had to extricate them by cutting them out of their clothes

c. bystanders' efforts to help flood victims

4. In which paragraph did you find the information or details to answer question 3?

_____

_____ Number of correct answers

Record your personal assessment of your work on the Critical Thinking Chart on page 198.

Personal Response

What would you have done when you saw the wall of molasses bearing down on you?

_____

_____

_____

Self-Assessment

I'm proud of how I answered question # _____ in section _____ because

_____

_____

_____

CRITICAL THINKING

Compare and Contrast

Think about the articles you read in Unit Three. Choose the four disasters that you feel were most frightening for those who experienced them. Write the titles of the articles that tell about them in the first column of the chart below. Use information from the articles to fill in the empty boxes in the chart.

Title	What happened to the people involved in this disaster?	What was the most frightening part of it?	Could it happen again? What could be done to prevent it?

Choose five disasters from this unit and rank them from least to most serious. Explain what standards you used to rank them. _____

_____

_____

Words-per-Minute Table

Unit Three

Directions: If you were timed while reading an article, refer to the Reading Time you recorded in the box at the end of the article. Use this words-per-minute table to determine your reading speed for that article. Then plot your reading speed on the graph on page 196.

Lesson No. of Words	15 1074	16 1232	17 1050	18 989	19 1040	20 939	21 913	Seconds
1:30	716	821	700	659	693	626	609	**90**
1:40	644	739	630	593	624	563	548	**100**
1:50	586	672	573	539	567	512	498	**110**
2:00	537	616	525	495	520	470	457	**120**
2:10	496	569	485	456	480	433	421	**130**
2:20	460	528	450	424	446	402	391	**140**
2:30	430	493	420	396	416	376	365	**150**
2:40	403	462	394	371	390	352	342	**160**
2:50	379	435	371	349	367	331	322	**170**
3:00	358	411	350	330	347	313	304	**180**
3:10	339	389	332	312	328	297	288	**190**
3:20	322	370	315	297	312	282	274	**200**
3:30	307	352	300	283	297	268	261	**210**
3:40	293	336	286	270	284	256	249	**220**
3:50	280	321	274	258	271	245	238	**230**
4:00	269	308	263	247	260	235	228	**240**
4:10	258	296	252	237	250	225	219	**250**
4:20	248	284	242	228	240	217	211	**260**
4:30	239	274	233	220	231	209	203	**270**
4:40	230	264	225	212	223	201	196	**280**
4:50	222	255	217	205	215	194	189	**290**
5:00	215	246	210	198	208	188	183	**300**
5:10	208	238	203	191	201	182	177	**310**
5:20	201	231	197	185	195	176	171	**320**
5:30	195	224	191	180	189	171	166	**330**
5:40	190	217	185	175	184	166	161	**340**
5:50	184	211	180	170	178	161	157	**350**
6:00	179	205	175	165	173	157	152	**360**
6:10	174	200	170	160	169	152	148	**370**
6:20	170	195	166	156	164	148	144	**380**
6:30	165	190	162	152	160	144	140	**390**
6:40	161	185	158	148	156	141	137	**400**
6:50	157	180	154	145	152	137	134	**410**
7:00	153	176	150	141	149	134	130	**420**
7:10	150	172	147	138	145	131	127	**430**
7:20	146	168	143	135	142	128	125	**440**
7:30	143	164	140	132	139	125	122	**450**
7:40	140	161	137	129	136	122	119	**460**
7:50	137	157	134	126	133	120	117	**470**
8:00	134	154	131	124	130	117	114	**480**

Minutes and Seconds

Plotting Your Progress: Reading Speed

Unit Three

Directions: If you were timed while reading an article, write your words-per-minute rate for that in the box under the number of the lesson. Then plot your reading speed on the graph by putting a small X on the line directly above the number of the lesson, across from the number of words per minute you read. As you mark your speed for each lesson, graph your progress by drawing a line to connect the X's.

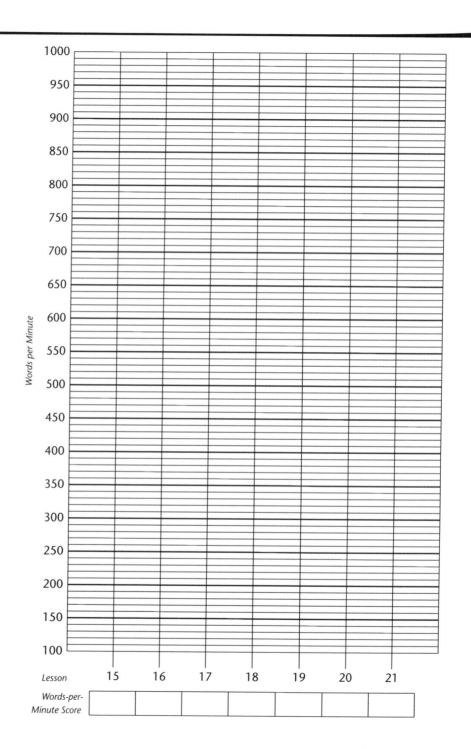

Lesson	15	16	17	18	19	20	21
Words-per-Minute Score							

Plotting Your Progress: Reading Comprehension

Unit Three

Directions: Write your Reading Comprehension score for each lesson in the box under the number of the lesson. Then plot your score on the graph by putting a small X on the line directly above the number of the lesson and across from the score you earned. As you mark your score for each lesson, graph your progress by drawing a line to connect the X's.

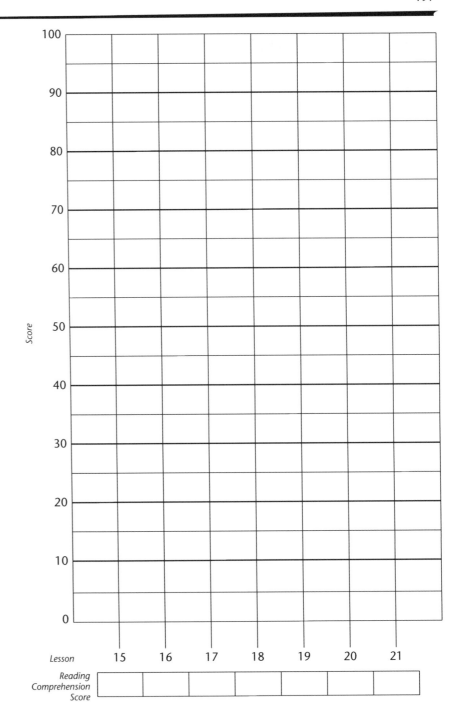

Plotting Your Progress: Critical Thinking

Unit Three

Directions: Work with your teacher to evaluate your responses to the Critical Thinking questions for each lesson. Then fill in the appropriate spaces in the chart below. For each lesson and each type of Critical Thinking question, do the following: Mark a minus sign (–) in the box to indicate areas in which you feel you could improve. Mark a plus sign (+) to indicate areas in which you feel you did well. Mark a minus-slash-plus sign (–/+) to indicate areas in which you had mixed success. Then write any comments you have about your performance, including ideas for improvement.

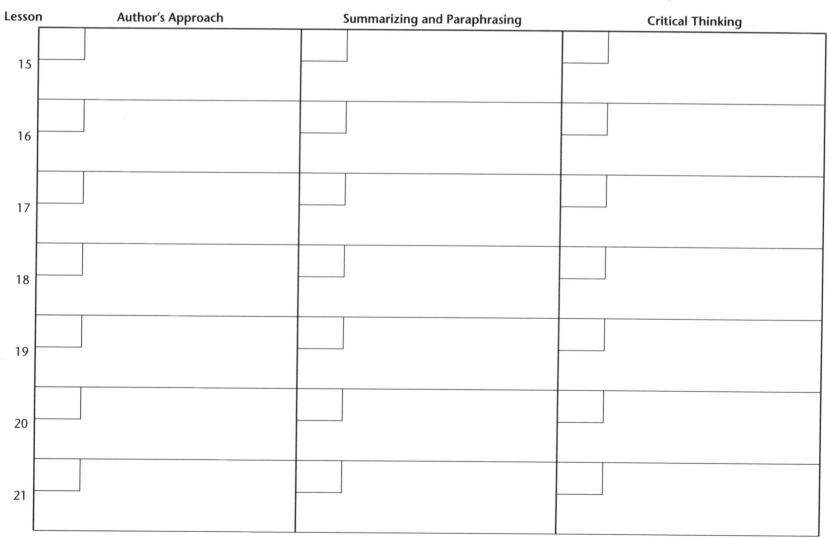

Lesson	Author's Approach	Summarizing and Paraphrasing	Critical Thinking
15			
16			
17			
18			
19			
20			
21			

Photo Credits